Paranormal
NEWCASTLE

Tyne Bridge and the Gateshead Sage.

Paranormal
NEWCASTLE

GORDON RUTTER

One of the many guard towers in Newcastle's walls.

First published 2009

The History Press
The Mill, Brimscombe Port
Stroud, Gloucestershire, GL5 2QG
www.thehistorypress.co.uk

British Library Cataloguing in Publication Data.
A catalogue record for this book is available from the British Library.

ISBN 978 0 7524 4917 3

Typesetting and origination by The History Press
Printed in Great Britain

CONTENTS

ACKNOWLEDGEMENTS

My thanks must go to my mother Kathleen and my wife Alison, both for generally putting up with me and also for practical help during this project. Thanks also to Gail-Nina Anderson, Michael Hallowell, Kay Easson, Tony Liddell, Rod Dickinson for his Air Loom 2002 photograph and to everyone else who has given me their take on some of the aspects of paranormal Newcastle. Many libraries were visited, in particular the National Library of Scotland, the Literary and Philosophical Society and also the National Records Office at Kew had much of interest. And to Paddy the cat, thanks for nothing.

My gratitude to all at The History Press, in particular Matilda Richards, Beth Amphlett and Alex Bud.

All photographs are copyright of Gordon Rutter.

INTRODUCTION: NEWCASTLE THROUGH THE AGES

ORIGINS

Naturally there has not been a city on the north side of the Tyne named Newcastle for time immemorial. The origins of what we now know as the city of Newcastle-upon-Tyne date back some 2,000 years, to the time of the Roman occupation.

ROMAN NEWCASTLE

For the Romans of AD 120, the site of Newcastle was pretty much just a bridge with a fort guarding it – this was called *Pons Aelius*. *Pons* is the Latin for bridge and *Aelius* is the family name of the Emperor Hadrian so we have 'the Bridge of Hadrian,' the name referred to both the bridge and the fort.

Initially the fort was wooden in construction, but by AD 150 a stone version had been erected. This Bridge of Hadrian was near to the end of Hadrian's Wall, which was a massive structure spanning the country from Carlisle to Newcastle and keeping two cultures apart. To the south of the wall were the Romans occupying England, and to the north were the Picts or, as we now know them, the Scots. Within Newcastle, Hadrian's Wall ran roughly west to east through the city along the line of what is now Westgate Road – this road was built on what was a defensive ditch just north of the Wall.

Pons Aelius originally marked the eastern end of Hadrian's Wall, but eventually it was extended another three miles to the North Sea at Wallsend where a fort named *Segendunum* was built.

The original *Pons Aelius* bridge is believed to have been made of wood with stone supports and it lasted much longer than the Roman occupation. Archaeological evidence suggests that it was not until 1248 that the wooden structure was eventually destroyed in a fire. The stone supports that had acted as a base for the wooden Roman bridge continued to be used for many years and now the iconic Swing Bridge (built 1876) occupies the approximate site. During the construction of the Swing Bridge two Roman altars were dredged from the Tyne: these were altars to the gods Neptune and Oceanus.

Mural showing historical periods of Newcastle, starting with the Roman fort and bridge, *Pons Aelius*.

Westgate Road, former location of Hadrian's Wall.

Swing Bridge and Tyne Bridge.

At the site of the *Pons Aelius* fort it is likely that there would have been a village, although no remains have ever been found. One kind of evidence for the Roman occupation has been frequently encountered at the site of the central railway station: coffins. It would appear that the station site covers the old Roman cemetery. The last mention of *Pons Aelius* is in AD 400 in a Roman document listing all territories and outposts of the Empire. Less than fifty years later the Western Roman Empire collapsed.

ANGLO-SAXONS AND NORMANS

The next peoples to make an impact on proto-Newcastle were the Angles who arrived in the area around AD 500. During the time of the Anglo-Saxons the area was known as Monkchester due to a community of monks that lived in the area. At this point in history Newcastle was part of the Kingdom of Bernicia. Eventually in the seventh century Bernicia combined with the Kingdom of Deira to form a much larger area called Northanhymbra, we now know this as Northumbria. During this period various monasteries were built at Monkchester and for a few years the Danish regularly sacked them, journeying up the Tyne for easy pickings. These communities never really grew to a large size. So for nearly the first 1,000 years of its existence Newcastle was just a small, relatively insignificant area with a few people and their homes and animals.

View of the Newcastle Swing Bridge over the Tyne (former site of *Pons Aelius*). The railway station and castle in background.

The statue of Neptune on top of Quayside restaurant, representing the Roman altar dredged from the River Tyne during the construction of the 1876 Swing Bridge.

Newcastle railway station from the top of the Keep.

THE NORMAN CONQUESTS

It was not until the Norman Conquests in 1066 that the Newcastle we know and love truly started.

After 1066 the Duke of Normandy, William the Conqueror's eldest son, Robert Curthose (c. 1054–1134), settled in the area. This move to the Tyne was as a direct result of a number of raids that took place both into and from Scotland. And in 1080 Curthose built a New Castle for the area.

The castle was built next to the still useable Roman bridge and the stunningly unimaginative but descriptive name has stuck ever since. The castle was of a motte and bailey form with a wooden tower on a mound of earth surrounded by a moat and wooden stockade. Over the years the castle grew in importance as a defensive area against Scottish incursion and over time a walled town built up around it; people moved into the area to service the garrison and the population continued to grow. As Newcastle grew in size and its military importance, trade and commerce increased in line with this, this fed back on itself giving, for a time, an almost exponential growth for the area.

A mural showing the importance of the sea to the development of Newcastle: Monkchester is shown as the next settlement after the Romans.

THE MIDDLE AGES

Due to its increasing size and proximity to the sea, complete with an easily navigable river, as the Danes had shown to the cost of all living at Monkchester, Newcastle rapidly became a major seaport. By 1300 Newcastle had achieved such prominence as a town that it was allowed to appoint its own mayor. By 1400 Newcastle (then with a massive population of 4,000) had become a county, independent of the county of Northumberland of which it had previously been a part, courtesy of Henry IV. The major industry of Newcastle from this time and for many centuries was the production and export of coal, chiefly to London. So well known was Newcastle for coal exports that the comparison of anything to the task of 'carrying coals to

Remnants of Newcastle's fortified walls.

Newcastle' is still used as a description of a useless task – although it must be said that the local coal industry has all but been destroyed. In the sixteenth century coal exports were 15,000 tons per year, by the mid-seventeenth century this had increased to 400,000 tons a year.

Shipbuilding was the second industry of the area (recorded since 1294) and rope and glass making were also important trades, as was the export of wool.

Obviously one of the key areas of Newcastle is the castle itself. The original castle built by Robert Curthose was on a defensive plateau overlooking the River Tyne and it was made of earth and timber. In 1172 Mauricius Caementarius rebuilt this castle out of stone, and he must have made a good job as much of the castle we see today is from this twelfth-century fortification. A later addition to the castle can also be seen: the barbican (an extension to a fortification, usually either a tower or a protective structure for a gate) which was added in 1215, known as the Black Gate. The Black Gate was eventually separated from the castle by the Victorian construction of the Newcastle to Edinburgh railway line which cuts directly between the two. Shortly after the construction of the Black Gate, the town of Newcastle was further fortified with the addition of city walls. These walls stretched around the area with a perimeter of two miles and they were a minimum of 7ft wide and 25ft high. Many parts of this wall still exist today. The walls contained six gates: Close Gate, New Gate, Pandon Gate, Pilgrim Gate, Sand Gate and West Gate and many of these names still exist even though there may be no sight of the wall of 1265. A smaller gate also still exists at an area called Sally Port: it was a gate next to the Tyne from which troops would sally forth against the enemy.

The Barbican or Black Gate of the castle.

Newgate as it is today, a former entrance to Newcastle through the city walls.

The Black Gate and St Nicholas Cathedral.

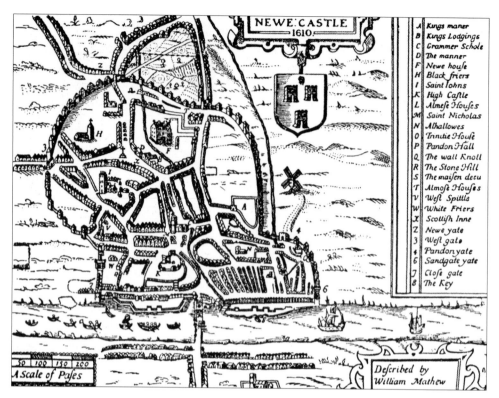

Map of Newcastle, 1610.

The walls had seventeen towers and a number of turrets and, as can be imagined, the whole was an impressive sight. Writing in the 1530s John Leland commented that they were 'far passing all the walls of the cities of England and most of the cities of Europe.' Other writers were equally impressed with Newcastle; William Brereton in 1635, described it as 'the fairest and richest town in England inferior for wealth and building to no city save London and Bristol.'

Near to the castle and Black Gate is the fourteenth-century St Nicholas' Church (built on the site of an eleventh-century wooden church), which became a cathedral in 1882 when Newcastle was granted city status. The religious life has been an important one in the development of the city of Newcastle and after Monkchester there have been many monasteries within the area of Newcastle.

At the start of the fourteenth century, Edward I, the Hammer of the Scots, brought the newly captured Stone of Scone and William Wallace through the town and, after Wallace's execution, by hanging, drawing and quartering, part of Wallace's body was displayed on the bridge across the Tyne.

THE KEEL MEN

One of the gates – Sand Gate – is a part of the quayside, an area which has recently seen great financial investment and regeneration. Sandgate (the name's modern form) was once the home of a Newcastle speciality: the Keel Men. They were responsible for taking coal from the riverside to the receiving ships and they got their name from the boats that they used which were capable of carrying up to 20 tons of coal at a time. The earliest recorded River Tyne use of a Keel boat is in the fourteenth century, but the word 'keel' has the distinction, apparently, of being the first English-language word committed to writing (a Welsh chronicler writing in the sixth century). The Keel Men lived outside the wall of Newcastle and fiercely protected their separate identity. Due to industrialisation and new techniques of loading coal, the Keel Men's jobs disappeared in the nineteenth century.

THE LOSS OF THE WALL AND THE COMING OF THE RAILWAY

By the late-eighteenth century the population of Newcastle had grown to over 20,000 and the walled area had become too small and so the suburbs of Newcastle started to appear as people built homes outside the wall. Eventually work began on the demolition of the wall and gates due to the disruption in the flow of traffic that they caused. This marked the beginning of a massive period of change for Newcastle.

From the start to the middle of the nineteenth century extensive modernisation and building work took place with many of the now familiar streets and buildings appearing (the architects of this scheme are commemorated in street names: Dobson, Grainger and Clayton). St Mary's Roman Catholic Cathedral was built at this time. And in 1853 the third (and worst) cholera outbreak to hit the city killed 1,533 people. Railways were becoming big business and Newcastle very quickly developed rail links with the rest of the country. The magnificent central railway station opened in 1850. In the 1870s the Town Moor was laid out as a series of parks and common-land areas. The iconic Tyne Bridge was opened in 1928 and by 1956 the last coal mine within the boundaries of Newcastle had closed.

MODERN NEWCASTLE

The most recent bridge to cross the Tyne (there are now six) opened in 2001 and it is called the Millennium Bridge. The population of Newcastle itself in the early years of the twenty-first century is roughly 260,000.

In 1974 Newcastle become a Metropolitan Borough. This extended the boundaries of Newcastle to include Benwell, Brunswick, Byker, Dinnington, East Denton, Elswick, Fawdon, Fenham, Gosforth, Hazelrigg, Heaton, Jesmond, Kenton, Longbenton, Newburn, Newcastle All Saints, Newcastle St Andrew, Newcastle St John, Newcastle St Nicholas, North Gosforth, Walker, West Brunton, Westerhope, Westgate and Woolsington.

GEORDIES

And one final thing on general history: the inhabitants of Newcastle are of course generally known as Geordies. This probably dates from the 1715 Jacobite Rebellion when Newcastle fought against the Old Pretender and declared its allegiance for King George I, so the inhabitants of Newcastle were proud to identify themselves as 'George's Men' or 'Geordies' for short.

A postcard of Newcastle railway station with the castle in the background.

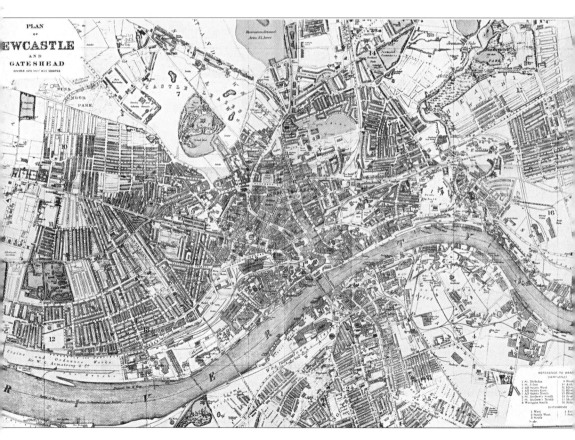

Map of Newcastle and Gateshead, 1890.

The iconic Tyne Bridge of Newcastle.

Modern Newcastle showing the many bridges crossing the Tyne.

Jesmond Dene.

The Old Mill, Jesmond Dene.

The ruined St Mary's in Jesmond Dene.

THE PARANORMAL

Unsurprisingly for a city of such great antiquity there have been many strange tales, and many of these are linked to the paranormal; this book covers some of the more interesting ones. But what is the paranormal? According to the *Collins Concise Dictionary* the paranormal is defined as anything 'beyond normal explanation.' It must be borne in mind that just because something is beyond normal explanation now, it doesn't always mean that will always be the case.

So we have a wide range of phenomena to look at, some are from the past but some are very much from the present and the tale of Paranormal Newcastle is still unfolding ...

Gordon Rutter, 2009

one

ANIMAL LIFE IN NEWCASTLE

There is a science which devotes itself to the study of animals that should not be there, it is called cryptozoology. Cryptozoology is the study of hidden, unknown or out of place animals. At one extreme we have the Loch Ness Monster and Bigfoot and at the other end of the spectrum we have a South American butterfly in Bognor. Not that the Loch Ness Monster often visits Newcastle and Bigfoot has never come closer to Newcastle than Bolam! But this doesn't mean that Newcastle doesn't have its own fair share of cryptozoological creatures.

THE BOOJUM

In 1913 Newcastle had a strange, cryptozoological visitor to the Jesmond Vale area. The animal in question was a Boojum. According to Lewis Carol, who resided twelve miles away from Newcastle in Sunderland for a time and gained many of his ideas for *Alice in Wonderland* from that city, a Boojum is a form of Snark. A Snark is an animal that was hunted by a motley crew of individuals in the nonsense poem *The Hunting of the Snark*. Regrettably none of the crew return from their expedition as the Snark was actually a Boojum. So a Boojum is a dangerous animal indeed. But what is a fictional animal doing annoying the good citizens of Jesmond?

Reports were issued from the area of a dog-like animal with what was described as a brindled back, pointy ears and a set of jaws that could open with a phenomenally large gape. Regrettably no pictures of the animal were forthcoming and the reports soon died off. It was seen for a few months, caused no damage, but frightened a few people and then it was not seen again.

So what was the Boojum? Clearly it was not an animal escaped from the imagination of Cambridge mathematics don, photographer and author Lewis Carol, or if it was Newcastle would surely also be plagued with white rabbits permanently late for their appointments! If we look at lists of British and European animals, none really fit the bill. We have to cast our Boojum net a lot wider before we find something to match. In Australia, Tasmania and New Guinea there lived an animal called a thylacine (also know as the Tasmanian Tiger). A thylacine is a medium-dog-sized marsupial with the ability to almost dislocate its jaw, so wide can it open it. In addition, the thylacine also has a straight tail, sticking out, but more importantly the hind quarters of the thylacine are quite markedly striped. There is no other known animal that fits the description. Unfortunately the thylacine is now extinct. The last know individual died in Hobart zoo in 1936. But prior to this, individual thylacines had featured in zoos and travelling menageries. Whilst it has become a cliché to say that unusual and out of place animals are escapees from travelling shows and zoos, it seems that this may well have been the case here. In the previous year just across the Tyne at Gateshead there had been much debate about travelling menageries visiting the area and being quite poorly looked after. As a result of this poor upkeep many of the animals frequently escaped and caused havoc until their recapture. Was the Boojum a case of an escaped thylacine? In the nineteenth century exactly this scenario was played out in the Lake District. A thylacine escaped and survived well in the area, hunting sheep, it soon earned the nickname of the Girt Dog of Ennerdale. It was not until it was actively hunted, shot and torn apart by dogs that the Lake District thylacine was laid to rest. The taxidermied thylacine was put on display in Keswick Museum until the 1950s when it was thrown out as being too moth eaten.

So we have an animal that fits the description. We have a proven means for the animal finding its way to Jesmond. We have scenarios for the subsequent cessation of sightings (recaptured by the travelling menagerie who wished to keep it quiet or moving on or eventually dying in an out-of-the-way-area). So why was it named a Boojum? Well those writing the reports would have been brought up on the poems of Lewis Carol and the description of the animal certainly suggests something fearsome and, as every good copy writer will tell you, nothing sells a story like a snappy name or title. So the Jesmond Boojum was created and then rapidly passed into history. Of course such incidents of dangerous animals escaping are mere things of the past that we need not concern ourselves with on a daily basis in the twenty-first century. Except…

ALIEN BIG CATS

On 18 October 2005 the Benton Campus of the University of Northumbria was the location for a similar sighting to that of the Boojum. Several members of library staff watched a large animal in the long grass. Their description was of a large cat with a long brown tail, a body light brown to cream in colour with a head a bit darker. The head was also described as small for the size of the body; overall the animal was described as being the size of a large dog (but quite importantly not the shape). The observation lasted for several minutes so the staff of the University had quite a prolonged sighting with plenty of time to study the beast. No photographs were taken of the animal in question. This is a fairly typical report of what is termed an alien big cat (an ABC), alien in the sense of a non-native to the locale rather than otherworldly! No other reports of an ABC have come from Newcastle itself but there are reports from the surrounding area, perhaps a case of curiosity getting the cat to move to pastures new?

Prudhoe (twelve miles from Newcastle) had two reports at Ovington of a big cat in 2003. Writing in 2007 for the Big Cats in Britain Group annual report, Ian Bond wrote:

> From the quality of some of the reports there is good reason to believe that there are, or have
> been recently, Big Cats of at least three different species at large in the North East. What seems
> equally as clear is that these are largely isolated individuals and, even allowing for the occasional
> breeding event, this is a population that would be described in any other circumstances as critically

The Old George, a haunted pub and location of a puma sighting.

endangered or even effectively extinct. In my opinion, whether we continue to have Big Cats in the North East depends either on future surreptitious releases or whether there are viable populations of these animals in other parts of the country from which individuals could disperse into the region; whilst the former is always possible, the latter I think is very unlikely.

There is also historical precedent for ABCs in the area. In the seventh century Newcastle did not exist as a named city and Tyne and Wear was merely a gleam in some nascent town planner's eye. The area we now know as Newcastle was part of Northumberland and it is from here that we have a record of some interest. The Venerable Bede (AD 673–735) wrote that in Northumberland one of the jobs of the shepherds was to guard their flocks from lions. Lions, in Northumberland in the seventh and eighth centuries, whatever next?

The incidence of big cats in the city of Newcastle itself is thankfully rare (one reported so far) but there are many reports from the surrounding area. Sergeant Eddie Bell, Durham Police's Wildlife liaison officer, estimated in 2001 that there were something in the order of fifteen big cats on the loose in the North East.

There has been one unequivocal sighting of a Big Cat in Newcastle however. It happened in the Old George Public House (a haunted pub) in the late 1960s. A number of people were in the pub drinking when another customer walked in. As pubs were a lot more relaxed then, this new customer thought nothing of bringing his pet into the pub. The other customers did however think something of it. The pet in question was a puma with a chain for a leash. The barman quite happily served the gent, who settled down to drink his pint, much to the shock of all the customers. It must be said that the barman had not seen his latest customer arrive and when he served him he was blissfully unaware of the extra guest, as it was hidden below the level of the bar, was out of his line of sight. The man and his puma were part of the visiting Newcastle winter zoo, which used to set up its home in the Old Town Hall in the Bigg Market.

OUT OF PLACE ALLIGATORS

An out-of-place animal of another variety was recorded in 2000. In the north-east of the city lies Heaton Park, a pleasant enough park for a walk, complete with a pond. But at the end of February 2000 police received a number of bizarre reports, reports that they would have dismissed as hoaxes were it not for the fact that there were several telephone calls. The reports stated that the witnesses had seen, in the pond, a 6ft-long alligator. Police called in some reptile experts from the Reptile Trust, Burnopfield, County Durham, who, after reading all of the reports, stated that the testimonies seemed to indicate the presence of a spectacled caiman alligator, more normally encountered in South America.

The trust also stated that the previous summer they had received three separate alligators from across Tyneside, including one which had been abandoned in a cardboard box outside the Tynemouth Sealife Centre. All three were 3ft long and possibly from the same batch of eggs. Another year and they would have been 6ft long – was it possible this newest denizen of Newcastle was from the same batch?

The reports had all originally been telephoned in to local radio station Metro FM, who passed the information on to the police. In such matters of course the police have to err on the side of caution and consequently they took the reports seriously. Peter Heathcote, chief executive of the Reptile Trust, said:

> There have been no other reports of the creature since those made to the radio programme. Unfortunately we have not been able to talk to any of the witnesses, so we don't know whether this is a hoax or not. But we have had caiman alligators abandoned recently and we had to take these reports seriously after we were contacted by the police. If the creature had been living in the water, there is little chance of it still being alive because of the cold temperatures.

The search was eventually scaled down after a lack of success and it seems that this was nothing more than a series of prank calls. One of the problems with any aspect of the paranormal is that not everyone takes it seriously and some think it is fair game to hoax people and to make up stories. This muddies the water somewhat and makes it even harder to prove and investigate to see if tales are true.

FURTHER AFIELD

One Newcastle resident who takes cryptozoolgy very seriously is Andrew Sanderson. Sanderson, along with Stockport-based colleague Adam Davies, has made several visits to Sumatra in search of a cryptozoological animal: the orang pendek. The orang pendek is reportedly a relative of the Himalayan Yeti and the North American Bigfoot, it is supposed to be an ape that walks upright on two feet but it is only about 5ft tall (a lot shorter than Bigfoot). On a 2001 trip the pair found footprints and hair samples. They were able to take a plaster cast of the best footprint and they had the hair samples analysed by a primatologist at Cambridge University. It's normally at this point in the tale that the scientist identifies the samples as from something relatively common in the area, but this time the scientist was unable to make a match with any known species. A return visit in 2004 found the pair close in on the trail of their quarry: a village they visited had seen him only two days earlier. Adam Davies said:

> [The villagers] said they had seen it eating soft fruit in farmland on the edge of their village. The orang pendek is said to have red-brown hair and walk like a man … and, two days later, one of our Indonesian guides heard it calling … we set after it and found new prints which we made casts of and which matched the prints which we discovered on our last trip. The prints had been made that day, our guides told us, and we also heard it calling, but were unable to capture it on film as it was in dense jungle. But I think we were at least within 500 metres of it.

Adam Davies subsequently returned to Sumatra in 2007 where he was able to collect more footprints. It might not be a Newcastle-based mystery animal but at least a Newcastle resident is living the dream and acting as a real-life Indiana Jones; who knows one day the Newcastle museums service may proclaim him as the discoverer of a new species of ape!

THE DEATH BADGER

One cryptic message about unknown or out-of-place animals was posted to an online cryptozoololgy notice board in 2000; it simply read, 'Has anyone ever heard of the Newcastle Badger of Death?? I've live [sic] in the North East and it was a common story when at school.' The poster, who named himself Fogofthetyne, was asked to elaborate but nothing more was ever heard from him. Perhaps a hoaxer or perhaps the Badger of Death wanted to be left in peace and wreaked its terrible revenge on Fogofthetyne for trying to thrust it into the limelight!

two

A CITY'S PASSIONS -
FOOTBALL AND RELIGION

BEND IT LIKE GELLER

One of the passions of Newcastle is, of course, football and specifically Newcastle United Football Club (NUFC) or, more colloquially, the Toon Army. Newcastle FC generally hover in the middle of the Premier division, not quite winning it but not in danger of relegation either. It's almost as if they have a charmed life, keeping them permanently in the public eye. But sometimes this charm appears to fail and Newcastle United have to do everything in their powers to rescue the situation.

At one time Newcastle did have help from powers other than those of Kevin Keegan and the other myriad players and managers to have graced the club over the years. During a run of poor results the team were at their wits end when someone had the bright idea of enlisting the help of none other than fabled spoon-bender Uri Geller himself. In 1996 Geller claimed to have influenced the result of the 15 June Euro 96 football match between England and Scotland. A penalty was being taken and Geller claimed that at the last moment he made the ball wobble, throwing off the aim of the redoubtable Gary McAllister, thus causing Scotland to lose the match 2–0. This and various other claims of Geller interventions in football matches (something not ruled against in the football code of conduct) reached the ears of someone working at the local newspaper, the *Evening Chronicle*. And the staff of the *Chronicle* hit upon the bright idea of getting Geller and his paranormal powers to lift the team out of their goal drought.

The specific problem was that by 2001 Newcastle had lost a run of twenty-nine consecutive London-based matches. For the 18 December match Newcastle journeyed to Highbury Stadium to play Arsenal. As they were playing, Uri Geller was running around the outside of the stadium to ensure a Newcastle victory. Geller subsequently claimed to have ensured that Arsenal's Ray Parlour was sent off and to have helped Alan Shearer curve a ball into the goal during a penalty. By the end of the match Newcastle were victorious with an historic 3–1 win. Arsenal manager Arsen Wenger was reported to have said that it felt like 'there was a sorcerer at work.' This win sent Newcastle to the top of the Premier league.

Afterwards, when asked about Newcastle's success Geller replied, 'I put my heart into it. It was incredible. I knew the team would win. I am so happy for everyone who supports them. It was exactly what I said.' This was their first London win since 1997 and for the first thirty minutes it

St James' Park, Newcastle United Football Club's home ground.

had looked as if Newcastle would lose this one as well. This was explained by Geller, 'I arrived late and had no ticket. But the moment I got out of the car and touched the Highbury stadium the Arsenal player Ray Parlour was sent off.' It must in all fairness be mentioned that Geller admitted he had help in turning Newcastle's fortunes around. Prior to the match a picture of Geller had been published in the *Evening Chronicle*. The plan for Geller to help the team to victory was outlined and people were asked to look at Geller's picture and grant him the power to accomplish the deed. Geller was also armed with a Newcastle scarf, shirt and football to concentrate his thoughts. Geller says that he 'started screaming and shouting for Newcastle to win. And soon after the start of the second half I said to my friend that Shearer would score from a penalty. That was half an hour before it happened. But I knew it. I knew the team would win.' It must be pointed out that at that time Shearer would have been the obvious penalty taker, and this was only said to Geller's friend – presumably if Shearer had not scored from a penalty then Geller would have kept quiet about his conversation with his friend. Geller also claimed that:

> Whilst Newcastle were scoring their winning goals I was running round the outside of the ground eleven times to lift the hoodoo. I even predicted the 3-1 score line after I got to the ground. I sat in the car and listened to the game on the radio. And after Arsenal scored I decided it was time to act. There was a lot to do with the number eleven. Newcastle had not won in twenty-nine games and two plus nine is eleven. Number eleven is very mystical and powerful. So I ran around the ground eleven times. The facts speak for themselves.

Often claims of success of psychics are given out retrospectively, but here we have a much-attested-to instance where it was widely publicised that Geller would change the fortunes of

Newcastle United, and they did indeed win. A shame he did not think of predicting the score in the paper as well, it would have been much more impressive to have said it several days in advance to a multitude of readers rather than during the match to a friend. Sad to say Uri Geller wasn't the first choice of the *Evening Chronicle* to lift the doldrums from Newcastle. They started off with an exorcist called David Fallcus, but he failed. Next came the turn of two American witch doctors – Papa Booga and Papa Jo, but they fared no better. Even the *Evening Chronicle* staff had tried – prior to a Worthington Cup match with Chelsea the *Chronicle* flew two stuffed magpies (Newcastle United are called the Magpies due to their black and white strip) 350 miles in a private jet. The idea was the dead birds would bring their namesake team good luck. They didn't. And only then did the *Chronicle* call in Geller.

THE BAD LUCK CONTINUES …

But it transpires that the bad luck of Newcastle United is not over yet. In 2008 a report in the *Sun* newspaper told that the club were still hexed due to a negative aura encircling them. Trevor Brown, an expert in curses and the paranormal, reckoned that the only way to save the club was by moving toward positive thought. According to Brown:

> Curses are all about negative thoughts. You can sense the atmosphere. And when you have 50,000 thinking the same thing, that is the outcome… it's like a whirlwind of negative energy. But as soon as Mike Ashley leaves and Kevin Keegan comes back the whole thing will turn around. If you hate something so much and you keep thinking it, that negative energy will take over. It is possible the club is cursed right now. But it will lift once the thought patterns change. If the right man comes in, it could go overnight.

So there we are. All Newcastle United needs is a manager their fans actually want and they will start winning games again. Or they could call Uri Geller back to the squad.

Newcastle United and the players do seem to have more than a passing acquaintance with Uri Geller, as in 2007 Newcastle defender Ben Haim decided to transfer to Chelsea, but only after he had consulted with Geller for advice!

IT'S ALL IN THE STARS

Another interaction of the paranormal and football was the fact that at the end of 2007 an astrologer took a look at NUFC. North-East astrologer Barbara Palliser cast a birth chart for the team and apparently, because there was a conjunction between Jupiter and Pluto as Pluto was leaving Sagittarius, the twelve months to December 2008 would be full of change. Shortly after the chart was cast, Newcastle manager Sam Allardyce was sacked and Kevin Keegan (former player, manager and all round Newcastle golden boy) was brought in to replace him.

The birth date taken for Newcastle United was 9 December 1892 which was the date that the team were actually given their name. Wouldn't this be a bit like casting an astrology chart based on your date of christening rather than date of birth? However, in all fairness what other date could you choose – should it be when it was decided Newcastle should have a team, the date of the first match, the date the first player was signed, etc? So in all probability it's as good a date as any to choose.

Palliser then cast a chart for new manager Keegan and compared it to that of the team. This comparison showed Mars as an important planet connecting the two charts. At the time this was done Mars was in retrograde motion in the skies (due to the interplay of the orbit of the planets at certain times, planets can appear to move backwards through the night sky as observed from the Earth). Retrograde planets like this are astrologically a sign of repeats so we have the repeat of Keegan as manager to Newcastle, a position he had held from 1992 to 1997. Palliser predicted that March 2008 would be the start of an important new phase in the history of the club and that this would probably be characterised by 'freedom. It symbolises a no-strings, maverick-type energy running through situations, and is recognisable by the highly charged, unpredictable atmosphere it activates.' This chart was posted online in March 2008 and in September Keegan resigned from his position due to disagreements with the owners of the club. In a September posting, at the time of the resignation, Palliser pointed out that March had signalled an end to Newcastle's latest losing streak and she then returned to continue to analyse the combined charts. After looking for meaningful conjunctions Palliser wrote:

> What was immediately apparent in Keegan's chart was that his Saturn in the sign of Libra was being activated by a number of planets currently crossing that point just as rumours started bubbling about what was taking place. Saturn relates to issues around authority, bosses, managers, limits and laws, while the sign of Libra, whose symbol is the scales, is concerned with relationship, with balance, harmony, justice and equality. Keegan is speaking Saturn in Libra when he gave his main reason for leaving: 'It's my opinion that a manager must have the right to manage and that clubs should not impose upon any manager any player that he does not want.'

The charts showed that mid-October would be a significant time for both team and ex-manager and she predicted that we had not seen the last of Keegan at Newcastle. Well nothing happened in mid-October. Joe Kinnear was appointed manager after Keegan's departure and he continued in that position through to the end of 2008 and beyond. Palliser felt that Keegan would be reinstated and another former Newcastle saviour, Alan Shearer, would join with him. As previously stated, Kinnear held the job from September on and he did indeed offer Shearer a position, as a member of the coaching staff, but Shearer turned it down. Palliser is still tipping both Keegan and Shearer in managerial roles. And for the end of the 2008/9 season Shearer accepted the role of manager.

But not all sports teams are as broad minded as Newcastle. One Newcastle-based paranormal investigator, Dean Maynard, has claimed to use his powers in the same way as Geller. Maynard claims to have already helped six different sports teams to success. These teams include (starting in 2005) the Chicago White Sox, who won the World Series for the first time in eighty-seven years, Darlington, which won after a losing streak of eight matches and Reading, which was promoted for the first time in their history. Maynard's first success was with Sunderland Football Club, as he says:

> Just over a year ago one of the players saw a ghost at Sunderland's ground and after that they had the most miserable luck. I went down there and did what I do and they started winning again. After that other people started contacting me and I would say 99 per cent of the time it works … I know it sounds strange, I carry out a ritual before the game and think positively.

But at heart Maynard is a huge rugby fan, in particular Maynard is a follower of Wigan Warriors. In June 2006 the Warriors were at the foot of the rugby league table and Maynard offered to change their fortunes. All he asked for in return were a couple of complementary tickets to the match. Wigan Wanderer's are not as forward thinking as Newcastle as a spokesman reported, 'We'd like to thank him very much for his kind offer but it's not something the club would be interested in.' Without Maynard's help Wigan won by 24 point to 18.

A TALE OF A HOLY WELL

A Holy Well is usually a spring of water which is believed to possess miraculous, usually healing, powers. Over time most Holy Wells are built up and often dedicated to a local saint (although many predated Christianity, Christian saints were attached to them). In general people at a Holy Well would come and partake of the sacred waters, drinking or bathing depending on the well, and often a votive offering would be left. And of course as befits a city of the status of Newcastle there is indeed a Holy Well.

Over the years many wells have been lost to the ravages of time, some have merely fallen out of use and subsequently they have dropped out of memory too. A precious few wells have been preserved, usually by locals, perhaps a person here or there popping down every so often to clear the area out. The Newcastle Holy Well, St Mary's Well, falls into this category and a rather

St Mary's Holy Well.

Signs of recent worship at the ruins of St Mary's Church, Jesmond.

splendid example exists in Jesmond Dene. The well has a long-attested history: in 1428 a papal letter (by Pope Martin V) refers to miracles wrought at the Chapel of Our Lady of Jesmond (St Mary's Chapel). As the chapel and well are separated by only a few dozen feet it is probable that the miracles refer to cures from the well itself. The chapel dates from the twelfth century, but it is now in ruins; this does not, however, stop it being used by some for worship even now. When last I visited, the area was festooned with flowers and various offerings and prayers were in place. There is no clear date for the building of the structure of the well (possibly seventeenth century), but legend has it that when a bathing place was added to the well in the early eighteenth century by William Coulson, the water ceased to flow. Eventually the water flow restarted as strongly as ever – perhaps it was a warning not to interfere?

The well is currently in a good state of repair, it was remodelled in the nineteenth century, and there is an arch, from under which the water bubbles up, with an inscription on it. The inscription was thought to read *Ave Maria Gratia Plena* (Hail Mary Full of Grace), but all that remains is the simple word *Gratia*. The current well structure dates from the seventeenth century as an archaeological excavation of the early 1980s demonstrated. Whilst no doubt some people still use the waters of the well for healing there are no clearly attested cases of a healing from modern times.

A MIRACLE IN WALKER

On the 10 October 1955 a small miracle was said to have occurred in the home of Theresa Taylor in Walker, Newcastle. A plaster cast of the Madonna started to weep what appeared to be tears. The weeping was first seen by Theresa as she was kneeling before it in prayer. First she saw the statue's left eye open and then a tear appeared in the corner of the eye. The event was witnessed by many neighbours of Theresa, but regrettably none of the tears were collected for testing and no photographs exist of the statue weeping.

THE PATRON SAINT OF NEWCASTLE

Talking of religious matters, how many of you can name the patron saint of Newcastle? Nope, it's a tricky one isn't it? The patron saint of the diocese of Hexham and Newcastle (the two areas were joined together in 1861) is none other than St Cuthbert. St Cuthbert's Day is 20 March. Born somewhere in the British Isles in 634 (according to some the son of an Irish king named Muriahdach), he eventually died on 20 March 687. Initially a shepherd, Cuthbert saw a vision of St Aidan of Lindesfarne being carried by angels and entering Heaven and this changed his life: he decided to become a monk and entered Melrose monastery at the age of seventeen.

Water source of St Mary's Holy Well, showing carving of Gratia in top stone.

Jesmond Old Cemetry.

The monastery at Melrose had been founded by St Aidan, but eventually Cuthbert and a number of other monks left Melrose (due to a change in liturgical practice) and moved to Lindisfarne. Cuthbert stayed there until 676 when he became a hermit on the Farne Islands, but he eventually returned to Lindisfarne in 685 (after much protesting) where he was made bishop.

Around this time Cuthbert, who was a noted healer, was working with plague victims and issuing prophecies. When he died of natural causes in 687 (having returned to his hermit's cave on the Farne Islands, he had foreseen his own death and decided this was where he wanted to die) Cuthbert was buried with the head of St Oswald, for safe keeping. I must admit I am not sure what they thought the dead Cuthbert could do to protect St Owald's head! The tomb of the saints rapidly became known as a place of remarkable miracles and St Cuthbert was called the 'Wonder Worker of England.'

In 698 the Holy Relics were moved and reburied and when this was carried out the body and head were found to be incorrupt (free from decay). Eventually in 875 the local monks fled a Danish Invasion and they carried the relics of the two saints with them. After seven years the monks were able to settle in a church at Chester-le-Street (some ten miles outside of Newcastle) which had been given to them by the Danish king. Eventually under fears of a fresh invasion in the tenth century our now well travelled saints were removed to Ripon in North Yorkshire. When the invasion failed to materialise after a few months the bodies were to be taken back to Chester-le-Street, but on the way the monks rested at Durham and due to the appearance of a miracle they decided that this was to be the final resting place of St Cuthbert. Eventually in 1104 Saint Cuthbert's body was finally placed in Durham Cathedral for good (there was a brief time since its first visit to Durham where it had been taken back to Lindisfarne). At this time his body and the head of St Oswald were found to be still incorrupt.

Statue of St Cuthbert holding
St Oswald's head.

Eldon Square Shopping Centre entrance, adjacent to Marks and Spencer, sight of a modern miracle.

Representations of St Cuthbert frequently show him carrying the incorrupt head of St Oswald. As well as being patron saint of Hexham and Newcastle, Cuthbert is also patron saint against plague (a useful saint for Newcastle as in the past they have endured a number of plague epidemics), shepherds and watermen. It is possibly the plague connection or the watermen association that earned St Cuthbert the Newcastle job as other than wandering around the area (dead or alive), he seems to have had no particular connection with the city.

THE MIRACLE OF NORTHUMBERLAND STREET

Miracles are often thought of as things of the past that don't happen anymore and definitely not in the middle of a city such as Newcastle. However, in July 2008 twenty-seven-year-old Ashley Huthart believes she was party to a miracle outside Marks and Spencer in Northumberland Street. Ashley's daughter, Celsee, who was three at the time, had hearing problems (requiring hearing aids), a symptom of a genetic disorder named Di George Syndrome, which is characterised by hearing problems, an inability to talk and heart and kidney issues. The pair were approached by a nun who touched Celsee's hand and blessed her. Ashley stated, 'It was amazing. She has had problems with her hearing since she was born but now she can hear everything. It is so strange. I have never believed in God or anything like that before but it must have been that. I'm going to go back and find that nun and say thanks.' Ashley and Celsee were on Northumberland Street merely killing time between hospital appointments, the final appointment of the day was to be a visit to their consultant at the Freeman Hospital. Accompanying the pair was Celsee's support worker who had spotted the nun collecting for charity. She had given Celsee some money to put in the nun's collecting tin and when she did the so nun said, 'Bless you' and touched Celsee's hand. At the Freeman Hospital it was found that Celsee had full use of her hearing. Ashley is still trying to locate the mysterious nun to thank her.

RELICS OF NEWCASTLE

One of the main streets in Newcastle is Pilgrim Street and there are various stories as to how it got its name. One explanation is that the street was the main thoroughfare for pilgrims on their way to St Mary's Chapel (and the Holy Well) in Jesmond. Another is that Greyfriars Friary (next to Pilgrim Street) held relics of St Francis, the founder of the Franciscans, and this would be the route pilgrims would take to visit the relics. The monasteries of Newcastle were dissolved during the reign of Henry VIII and any relics that were held within them were generally lost to the world. Of the many monasteries and nunneries that were present in the early years of Newcastle only the Blackfriars convent building survives to this day, at the dissolution it was rented out to nine separate guilds to use as their headquarters.

THE BLESSED VIRGIN MARY PUTS IN AN APPEARANCE

According to a local and ultimately unverifiable tradition the name of Jesmond comes from an apparition of the Blessed Virgin Mary. Prior to the 1066 Norman Conquests Jesmond had been known as Gese Muth which translates as the mouth of the Ouse, the Ouse being the river which flows through the area into the Tyne. Shortly after 1066 (date unspecified) a vision of the Blessed Virgin Mary was seen and she was holding the infant Christ, thereafter the area was known as the Hill of Jesus, which was translated and corrupted into Jesmond. The appearance is supposed to have taken place at St Mary's Rock in the river adjacent to where now stand the ruins of Ridley Mill.

An early twentieth-century postcard of Ridley Mill and St Mary's Rock, Jesmond, site of an ancient sighting of the Blessed Virgin Mary and Jesus.

St Mary's Rock – the site of an early appearance of the Virgin Mary.

The nearby St Mary's Chapel (now ruined) may have started life as a so-called slipper chapel where pilgrims would remove their footwear and continue barefoot to the rock of the apparition where they would venerate the Blessed Virgin Mary and Jesus. The ruined St Mary's Chapel was destroyed in the dissolution in the sixteenth century, but Mass is still occasionally said there by the local Roman Catholic Priest or the Bishop of Hexham and Newcastle. Outwith these services the church is frequented and visitors at any time can find flowers and small shrines that have been set up by the faithful.

THE EXORCISTS OF NEWCASTLE

In 2007 a Muslim cleric, fifty-one-year-old Hamidur Rahman of Elswick, from Newcastle's Shah Jalal Mosque, took his employers to an industrial tribunal over claims that they sacked him because of his out-of-hours work as an exorcist. It was claimed that he had set up a mobile-phone hotline for exorcisms and that he would carry these out and give out blessings over the telephone. After the threat of a court battle Rahman was given an out-of-court settlement of £17,500. Rahman said, 'I have been caused considerable distress by the dismissal and I am deeply offended I was called the Mobile Exorcist.' Rahman denied the claims and pointed out that he had not in fact owned a mobile phone for two years.

There are however Newcastle inhabitants who are definitely exorcists and proud of it. Local Radio DJ Alan Robson broadcasts on Metro Radio, which is based in Newcastle. Ever since November 2000 Robson has been a qualified exorcist (I'm not quite sure who hands out that qualification!). Robson performed the first ever exorcism broadcast on radio (as part of his Scary Christmas Show) and once held the world ghost hunt record for taking 2,554 people to different haunted venues in a single night. Robson has presented the Metro Radio Night Owls show since 1983 and he frequently takes his listeners to some of the scariest places on Earth. *Scariest Places on Earth* is also the name of a regular television show Robson presents for ABC television in the United States. As well as being a television and radio broadcaster and exorcist, Robson is also a pagan historian, although he is not himself a pagan.

Robson's interest in the paranormal and specifically exorcism can be traced back to his version of the conversion on the road to Damascus. Previously he had mocked those who saw ghosts but one day a church exorcist, after hearing the Night Owls show, invited Robson along to an exorcism. As Robson describes it:

> The first two places I felt nothing happening. But at the third he walked through the door and said, 'this might be too much for you.' Of course nothing else could have made me want to go in more. When I got in you could tell something was wrong. And then I saw all kinds of things, shadows and objects moving by themselves.

After that there was no turning back for Robson and he now reckons to perform on average one exorcism per week. Believing himself to be in tune with all things of a spirit nature Robson can tell straightaway if a house has a spirit presence just by its feel. He describes this as akin to walking into a home and knowing whether it is a happy house or not. Robson can be heard on Radio Metro Tuesday to Sunday from 10 p.m. to 2 a.m. and some of his more memorable shows are also archived online at Metro Radio.

three

MUMMIES OF NEWCASTLE

Over the course of relatively recent history Newcastle has had a bit of a thing for Egyptian mummies.

The first record of an Egyptian mummy in Newcastle dates from 1821. The Literary and Philosophical Society of Newcastle on Westgate Road (Lit and Phil) received from Thomas Coates esq. of Haydon Bridge, Northumberland, an Egyptian mummy in perfect preservation and, as it was described, of great beauty. The mummy originally came from Thebes and when it arrived at the Lit and Phil, it was still in its original coffin, which was beautifully decorated and the face that had painted on the outside of the coffin excited favourable comment from all who saw it. At the time of the presentation of the mummy James Ramsay, a noted portrait painter, was commissioned to produce a watercolour of the sarcophagus and its decorations. The mummy was found to be that of an Egyptian princess named Bakt Hor Nehkt and recent work by the Newcastle Museums service has produced a computer recreation of how she would have looked in life.

There is little record of what next happened to this mummy (until she was eventually housed in the Hancock Museum of Newcastle) but it was presumably well admired as in 1826 the Lit and Phil received another mummy. This one was presented to the society by John Bowes Wright after he had purchased it in 1825 from the sale of the goods of Baron Denon in Paris. Denon was the first Director of the Louvre Museum. The mummy had originally been discovered in 1798 at Thebes when Napoleon invaded Egypt. Some 2,500 years old, the mummy was called Irt Irw. Irt Irw arrived at the Lit and Phil on 8 March 1826 and the plan was soon hatched to open the mummy as part of a public display in 1830. Three surgeons, Greenhow, Baird and Fife, were to perform the operation. The records of the event tell us that the mummy was stored in two cases of sycamore wood, which showed good preservation. Firstly the surgeons removed the wrappings of the mummy which weighed 50lb in total. The body was described as being in a remarkable state of preservation, the hair was long and perfect with a reddish tinge although it did show signs of greying. Also in perfect condition were the teeth of the mummy and the breasts were described as large and pendulous and the skin as a whole was likened to a sepia brown. The mummy was described as being aged between thirty and forty years with no apparent cause of death. Once the mummy had been unwrapped and shown to all present it was then placed on display in the gallery in the library, stored in a glass case. Eventually Irt Irw

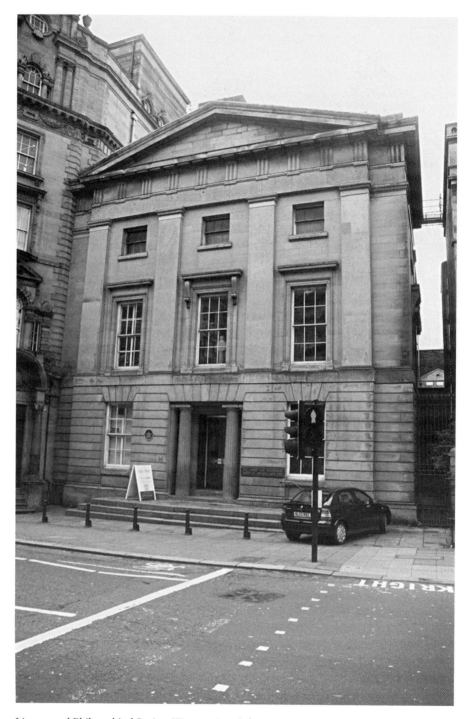

Literary and Philosophical Society, Westgate Road, first port of call for Egyptian mummies visiting the city.

Hancock Museum, location of moving mummies.

was housed at the Hancock Museum and during 2008 and 2009 a second autopsy was carried out to see if a cause of death could be established.

As stated, both mummies eventually found their way to the Hancock Museum, a local museum in the old tradition of a cabinet of curiosities (in other words a little bit of everything which was collected purely on the grounds of interest to Hancock). One of the mummies did not seem to be happy in the Hancock. Ever since the move there have been reports of a mummy moving around the museum at night. There is regrettably no solid documentary evidence for this. The Hancock closed for redevelopment recently to reopen, in 2009, as part of a much bigger museum: the Great North Museum. It will be interesting to see if the mummy settles down to its new home and stays put or if it continues its nocturnal wanderings. Whilst the £26 million redevelopment of the Newcastle museum takes place the mummies have been on display at the Segendunum Roman Fort at Wallsend. There have been no reports of mysterious mummy movements there!

four

GHOSTS, HAUTINGS AND SÉANCES

As you would expect with 2,000 years of inhabited history, the area of Newcastle appears to have a collection of ghosts. Newcastle has a fair number of ghosts and there are plenty of tales to amuse and enough to support several ghost hunting teams and a permanent ghost tour.

SPIRITS WITH SPIRITS – GHOSTS OF PUBLIC HOUSES

It is a curious fact that the majority of ghosts are of the relatively recently deceased, for example ghosts of dinosaurs and caveman are not encountered; the oldest reported ghosts in the country seem to be those of Roman soldiers. Newcastle's oldest ghost is the ghost of Charles I.

King Charles was captured by the Scots in 1646 and held in Pilgrim Street. As he was a king he was allowed certain privileges and one of these was the occasional round of golf at Shieldfield. Another privilege revolved around the return journey back to his prison – he was allowed to stop off at the Old George pub (presumably merely called the George then) for a drink. The pub now has a Charles I room and the chair which the king allegedly used is still extant and on display. Visitors have reported seeing the outline of a grey figure sitting in the chair: perhaps it is King Charles popping in for a swift half on the way somewhere.

Pubs appear to be full of all sorts of spirits – and not just the ones that the customers are after. Robinson's Wine Bar on the Cloth Market has the spirit of an Edwardian gentleman: a tall man seen leaning against a wall within the bar. The spirit has only been seen by the manager of the bar during the mid part of the twentieth century, so not the best bet for ghost hunters to see.

Another pub associated with a ghost is the Cooperage pub at the quayside, which is housed in a fifteenth-century timber-framed building. The Cooperage has not always been a pub. It spent time as a cooperage (of course), a private house, a warehouse and since 1973 a public house. Over the years many staff and customers have reported ghostly goings on. These reports have ranged from the ephemeral such as footsteps and movement seen from out of the corner of the eye through to full-body apparitions. Several consistent reports over the years at the Cooperage have included sightings of a faint figure in the restaurant, a man looking out of a window when the room is known to be empty, a young blonde-haired girl and, most bizarrely, a figure said to constantly change colour!

The Old George public house, current site of residence for the ghost of King Charles I.

Another ghost is also said to inhabit the alley next to the Cooperage. It is believed to be the ghost of Henry Hardwick, a cooper, who was attempting to flee a sixteenth-century press gang when he was caught in the alley. The press gang was not impressed at having been lead such a merry dance and rather than conscript Hardwick into service, they decided to beat him to death instead. In doing so they gouged out his eyes. Late at night the figure of Hardwick can still be seen with black sockets where the eyes should be.

Of course not all ghosts can be seen – and one of the mast famous categories of invisible ghost is the poltergeist. Poltergeists (from the German for noisy spirit) are ghosts which are normally attached to children and are basically mischievous spirits, responsible for practical jokes and damage of materials. Newcastle has a poltergeist attached to a pub, the Board Room public house of Stevenson Road. During the 1980s the landlord, Richard Bell, reported glasses shattering, pictures moving and furniture being disturbed. Since then, however, the poltergeist activity seems to have died down.

Some ghosts appear to behave somewhat differently to the way they behaved when they were alive. The La Dolce Vita Nightclub (now closed) of Low Friar Street had the ghost of a monk which was seen to be boogying the night away. A monk in a nightclub. Dancing. Strange indeed.

GHOSTS OF THE QUAYSIDE

Staying on the quayside (an area which has undergone much recent regeneration and financial investment), but moving away from public houses we have the ghost of Jack the Beadle at

The Cooperage public house, multiplicity haunted location.

Alleyway next to the Cooperage, said to be haunted by an eyeless ghost.

All Saints' Church. Jack the Beadle was a well-liked individual, but he came to a sticky end in 1858 when caught trying to steal lead from coffins, his ghost is still encountered at the scene of his crime. As a contemporary rhyme tells us:

If you want to rob the dead
Gan to Jack the Beadle
He's the one who steals the lead
Pop goes the weasel

The quayside is a popular place for ghosts, around John Wesley's Memorial the ghost of an executed murderer has been seen, a murderer guilty of the crime of matricide. The murderer, Jane Jameson, tried to frame her boyfriend, Billy Ellison, but she was executed for the crime in 1829 and her ghost now wanders the quayside area calling out his name. His ghost has not been sighted – understandably he seems to want nothing more to do with her!

We now have a faceless ghost, that of Martha Wilson, which is encountered around the Broad Chare area of the quayside. Martha Wilson was a suicide from 1817 who was buried at the nearby crossroads, the ghost of Martha has been encountered as a veiled woman and when approached she lifts the veil to show she has no face. Because of her clothes Martha Wilson is an example of a sub-group of ghosts called a silky. A silky is a Northumbrian based ghost with rustling silk garments. Some authors, such as Lewis Spence in *The Minor Traditions of British Mythology*, describe the silky as being a variant of the Irish banshee – a female spirit whose wailing cries are a warning of impending death!

The Quayside, location of hauntings of Jack the Beadle and Jane Jameson.

Broad Chare home to faceless ghost Martha Wilson – a Silky.

GHOSTS OF NEWCASTLE FORTIFICATIONS

Newcastle is, as previously stated, named after the New Castle built in the eleventh century by William the Conqueror's son – pleasingly the remains of the castle appear to have their own ghost. During a ghost vigil in May 2006 a 4ft tall black mass was photographed.

Another old ghost of Newcastle's fortifications is said to date from 1644. At Sallyport Carpenter's Tower (a thirteenth-century defence tower) there is the ghost of a soldier who died whilst fighting the Scots sometime between July and October 1644. Normally the ghost has been seen staring mournfully from a window of the Tower. One witness did see something slightly different: he watched the ghost slowly float up, eventually passing through the ceiling. Subsequent enquiries revealed that in that exact spot during the seventeenth century there had been a spiral staircase, a staircase which has now been dismantled. By all accounts this cavalier ghost is a very friendly spirit.

CHURCHYARD GHOSTS

A churchyard ghost inhabits one of the oldest churchyards of Newcastle, that of the mid-twelfth-century parish church of St Andrew on Newgate Street. At the start of the nineteenth century a young curate was having assignations with Charlotte, the daughter of a local landowner. After a quarrel they had parted on poor terms and the curate, after a day or two, resolved to see her to straighten things out. As he was about to leave to travel to her home he saw her walking through the churchyard, in her favourite blue dress and shawl. Naturally he ran to intercept her,

The Castle Keep at night where a *Most Haunted* television vigil reported all manner of paranormal happenings.

but equally naturally he was unable to find her. By the time that he had finished looking he decided it was too late to carry out his planned visit. The following day he discovered that just about the time he had seen her in the churchyard she had died at home.

Whilst photographing the church and churchyard for this book I found myself in conversation with a local. He told me the above story, which I already knew, but he added the fact that within the past couple of years a friend of his had witnessed the ghost and that he described her as a friendly spirit who meant no harm to anyone. Prior to this it had been assumed that the ghost had perhaps moved on as she had not been seen for a number of years.

St Andrew's was also involved with the Newcastle witchcraft trials. It received the bodies of at least fifteen executed witches, along with many criminals, but both groups seem remarkably quiet and peaceful and they don't appear to involve themselves in this haunting lark; unless of course one is responsible for the following tale. At the end of the eighteenth century a sexton mysteriously disappeared, only to be found the next day. Unfortunately he was not found alive and well, that would be too happy an end to this tale. Instead he was found at the bottom of a freshly dug grave, dead. It was reported that he had died of fright! What frightened him has never been recorded, but with such an illustrious content to their graveyard who knows what it could be …

Interestingly the church is open to many ideas and in 2008 they had the land dowsed and apparently discovered the remains of an older church directly beneath the current building (the main porch is the newest part of the current church and dates from 1726).

St Andrew's Church, burial place of murders and witches and home of ghosts.

Grave stone path at St Andrew's Church.

Early on in its history the church was funded by the sale of indulgences – an indulgence is essentially a get out of jail free card for sins. In fact one of the three chantries of the church, the Chantry of the Holy Trinity, was founded by Sir Adam de Athol, Lord of Jesmond and Sheriff of Northumberland in 1392. The presiding bishop said:

> That whoever offers or sends, or causes to be sent to the chapel of the Holy Trinity in the northern part of the same church, either gold, silver, vestments, books, chalices, or any other ornaments, which are wanting to the aforesaid chapel, or altar, or image of the Holy Trinity, which is in the same chapel – or who shall fall down upon their knees before the image of the Holy Trinity, aforesaid, and pray for the health of Sir Adam de Athol, knt (knight) as long as he lives, and for his soul after his decease, and for the soul of the Lady Mary his wife, whose body lies buried in the same chapel of the Holy Trinity, shall, as often as they perform those things, or any of the things before-mentioned, have the benefit of forty days indulgence.

In the early 1880s at St Nicholas' Cathedral (which at the time was merely a church) a tall shadowy knight would be seen walking around. When he wasn't seen, the sound of creaking armour was frequently heard. Regrettably this spirit has since disappeared and gone to wherever spirits move on to.

THEATRE GHOSTS

One of my favourite types of haunting is those of theatres. The Tyne Theatre on Westgate Road has a typical example of a theatre ghost. The Tyne Theatre and Opera House, as it was originally called, opened in 1867 complete with state-of-the-art special effects equipment. In particular the theatre had a rather ingenious thunder-making sound machine – a canon ball would be rolled down a piece of tin guttering producing the requisite noise. But regrettably on the night of 7 April 1887 a 36lb cannonball fell from the apparatus striking the head of thirty-year-old carpenter Robert Crowther. Crowther suffered a fractured skull and died instantly. From then on his ghost has been frequently encountered pushing past people and is occasionally found sitting in his favourite seat.

On several occasions cleaners have reported lights being switched on and off. In one incident a manager at the merchandise stand spotted a person in Victorian clothing walking through the foyer. Actors are not allowed to be seen by the public in costume except when they are on stage so the manager decided to have a quiet word with him, but as she approached, the figure vanished. Even when not seen Crowther's distinctive pipe smoke is often smelt. The ghost is referred to by staff as Bob and a rather interesting sighting was reported in 2000 when he was seen by stage staff on two successive Thursdays during the pantomime season. These appearances were quiet reassuring, as Bob had not been seen since the theatre had been badly damaged by fire in 1985.

But this is not the only theatre ghost in Newcastle: the Theatre Royal has one of its own too. The Theatre Royal, which opened in 1837, stands on Grey Street. The current building is not entirely original: the insides were severely damaged in a fire in 1889 (eventually reopening in 1901). But fortunately no one was killed in the fire so no ghosts were generated, but before that incident, in the 1880s, a fan of the theatre would frequent performances and afterwards she would wait at the stage door to collect autographs.

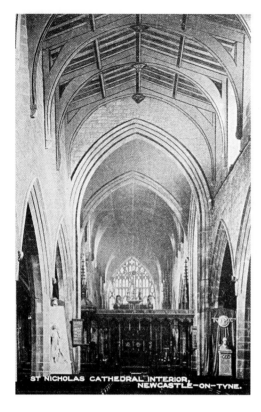

A postcard showing the interior of St Nicholas' Cathedral, where a ghostly knight was seen in the nineteenth century.

St Nicholas' Cathedral.

The Tyne Theatre location for a haunting by Robert Crowther, the only man killed by thunder.

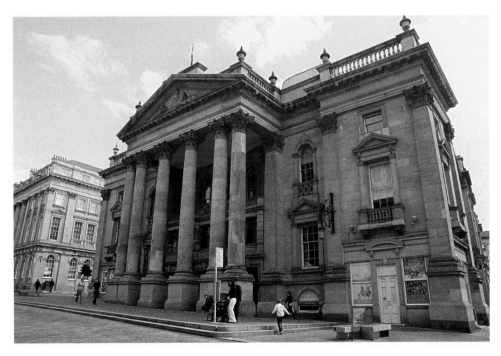

The Theatre Royal, a theatre with a ghost the result of unrequited love.

During one autograph session she caught the fancy of an actor who promised they would elope on the last night of the play. Unfortunately he was not quite true to his word and when he saw his fan on the last night of the play, ready to start a new life together, he merely laughed in her face. Somewhat overcome the spurned lover retired to the upper gallery to watch his play for one last time. At the appearance of her former beau she stretched out her hand as if to touch him, but she stretched too far and she plunged over the balcony to her death. Or possibly she threw herself from the balcony to commit suicide at having been spurned and so cruelly treated. As there was no one sitting next to her we will never know. Ever since then the ghost of a grey lady has been seen in the theatre. Regrettably the names of the principles in this sad tale of affairs have ben lost for posterity. But whoever the grey lady is she is not alone as there are a couple of tales of other haunted happenings at the Theatre Royal.

One member of staff was working in one of the boxes at the Theatre Royal when he heard a noise coming from the box above him, a box which should have been unoccupied. He went upstairs to investigate and sure enough there was no one there. After he had gone back downstairs to the box he was working in the sounds started up again and he rushed upstairs to try to catch the perpetrator in the act, again the box was empty, but this time all the chairs in the box had been overturned. A conscientious soul, he again returned to his box to continue his work, but this time he locked the door so no one could approach him unawares and he played the radio at such a volume as to drown out any sounds coming from the box above or from anywhere else.

One brief report I have found mentions an actress who committed suicide in the theatre in 1935 and it is said her ghost still wanders the area, but unfortunately I have been unable to find many extra details about her. The final Theatre Royal ghost is a female figure encountered in the gents' toilet. An electrician saw a woman in the toilets and assumed he had stepped into the wrong toilet, he apologised and left. But upon discovering that he was in fact at the correct toilet he re-entered to find that the woman had vanished.

Inspired by these ghost tales a ghost hunter group, Northern Ghost Investigations, staged an enquiry on 13 April 2007 starting at 11 p.m. and lasting through till 5 a.m. the following morning. Initially there was a tour of the premises, including the back-stage area, but the actual investigation was restricted to the audience seating area. The group was supported by several mediums who picked up on a number of spirits, including one who claimed to have been a manager at the theatre. Non-mediumistic investigators also experienced temperature fluctuations and heard the sound of breathing. A final séance at the end of the session produced nothing and the mediums all reported that the building was generally pretty quiet. To be honest that sort of report, whilst not exciting for the participants, is reassuring: if every investigation yielded results of a paranormal nature then the paranormal and ghosts would have been proven long ago. So negative results might tell us there is nothing there or they may just suggest that spirits are simply not there for our every beck and call.

RELIGIOUS GHOSTS

The oldest religious house in Newcastle (once Newcastle existed as a named entity) is that of the Benedictine nunnery of St Bartholomew, founded in 1135 on the site of what is now Grainger Market. One local street commemorates the fact in its name, Nun Street. Many other religious houses were founded in the same general area: Austin Friars, Carmelites, Dominicans and Franciscans were all there. Each was distinguished by the colour of their robes; the Dominicans, for example, were the Black Friars. The Black Friars were also commemorated in the name of the area and Blackfriars has a phantom Dominican friar. At the time when the following incident occurred two holy houses of Benedictine nuns (founded 1086) and Black Friars (founded 1239) were on opposite sides of Newgate Street. Rumour has it that they were linked by secret underground passages. On the western side was the friary and on the eastern side was the convent. Indiscretions occurred. A nun became pregnant. As a punishment she was walled up alive in the nunnery and her ghost is still said to wander Nun Street. There is no record of any punishment meted out to the monk, but there is record of a ghostly monk being seen disappearing in the cloisters of Blackfriars which are the remains of the monastery.

That was a ghost of a Dominican (a Black Friar). There's also a ghost of a Franciscan in Newcastle (a Grey Friar). This one is in an altogether more modern setting and one easily accessible as well: the Tyneside Film Theatre on Pilgrim Street. Initially the reports were vague: cleaners feeling uncomfortable, seeing undefined shapes and finding seats in positions different to the ones that they had been left in, but eventually the shear number of reports started to give even the most sceptical pause for thought. One of the front-of-house staff was checking

The Tyneside Film Theatre is home to a phantom-monk patron.

everything was ready for the evening's screenings when he too witnessed a shadow moving where it shouldn't have been. When he broached the subject with his colleagues he found that as well as the original reports, of which he had been openly sceptical, there were also sightings of a figure in monk's robes moving around the building and even people hearing the ghost clearing its throat. Next time you're in there and someone is blocking your view just be careful, it might be the Grey Friar ghost of the Tyneside Film Theatre.

VICTORIAN SÉANCES

In 1848 a new phenomenon swept the world and naturally, as now, it had its grounding in North America. Two sisters, Margaret and Kate Fox, living just outside New York (in a small town called Hydesville which is now the centre of spiritualism), had apparently found that they could communicate with the dead by a series of knocks and raps. They came up with a code – once for yes, twice for no with more complex communications spelt out by knocking out the appropriate number of the letter in the alphabet. This was the start of the religion of Spiritualism and it was also the start of the séance as an entertainment. Naturally many formal and informal séances were carried out; the following are some reports from the nineteenth century, followed by a modern version of a spirit investigation and séance.

One of the most famous groups performing séances throughout America were the Davenport brothers, Ira Erastus Davenport and William Henry Harrison Davenport. Happy with their success in North America the Davenports decided to break into new areas and chief amongst these was Europe. And so in November 1864 Newcastle saw the arrival of the Davenports for their own particular brand of séance. Twenty-six of Newcastle's great and good gathered at Baker's Temperance Hotel on Westgate Street. The events herein described are taken from a pamphlet published by one of the audience members, Mr T.P. Baker, subsequently proprietor of the Central Exchange News Room.

At the hotel the expectant audience were met by the Davenports and W.F. Fay, a twenty-five-year-old American who had been a practising medium for eleven years and Dr J.B. Ferguson who was to act as master of ceremonies of the whole proceedings. For some reason it is always said that ghosts prefer the dark so a darkened room lit only by a single chandelier was to be the venue. All told thirty people were present in the room along with the Davenport's distinctive spirit cabinet – a large roofless wardrobe-type affair with room for the two brothers to be bound in chairs. The two brothers could be housed in the cabinet in separate sections and items could be placed in the cabinet between them. The cabinet was examined before the evening's proceedings took place and when it had been agreed that it was exactly as it appeared (an empty, wooden, roofless cabinet), two volunteers securely tied the Davenports into chairs in the cabinet.

After the brothers were securely tied, the volunteers proceeded to place a range of musical instruments in with them. The lights were lowered to make the area more appealing for the spirits and in the darkness the audience heard the inner door of the cabinet lock (remember the Davenports were bound hand and foot by this time), the outer doors having previously been locked by the volunteers. Almost immediately a trumpet was thrown out. The lights were switched on and everything was found to be as before, the Davenports were still securely bound. The trumpet was then replaced and the proceedings continued. A guitar and tambourine were both heard to play before the trumpet was again thrown out. When checked upon, the Davenports were still bound. At this point they invited a member of the audience to join them inside the cabinet and the Revd Taylor was happy to oblige. The Revd Taylor sat between the two brothers at such a distance so that he was physically touching both brothers simply by being in the cabinet. Again instruments could be heard playing and when the doors were opened to check the tambourine was found to be on the Revd Taylor's head! The reverend gentleman confirmed that he had not felt the brothers move, but he also reported that he had felt a cold hand caressing his face. The Revd Taylor retired from his position and the cabinet doors were then closed and the audience heard the ropes being untied and the Davenports stepped out of the cabinet. And that was the end of the first part of the show.

For the second part of the séance the cabinet was dispensed with and two guitars and a tambourine were placed on the table (everyone had obviously decided the spirits did not like the trumpet as they kept throwing it out). The medium Mr Fay and Ira Davenport were tied together in chains and William Davenport and Dr Ferguson placed themselves amongst the audience. The audience were all holding hands and they had all agreed that there would be no lights during this performance. Remember the audience was made of such worthies as Joseph Cowen, who would soon be Newcastle's MP, and John Mawson, who would, in 1867, become the County Sheriff. So their word as gentlemen was of course to be trusted. As the lights were put out music started up and some members of the audience were hit around the head as the instruments moved about the room.

Despite the agreement for no lights the temptation for one audience member proved too much and a Mr Ward struck a match. As he did so the actions being felt around the room ceased. Ferguson was incensed. He demanded the immediate removal of Ward before the proceedings could continue. Ward merely observed that he had been checking for fakery and that when he had struck the match he saw William Davenport standing in the room. Mr Stephenson and Mr Mawson, who had been seated either side of William Davenport, maintained that at no point had he left his seat until after the match had been struck. As the match was struck they claimed that Davenport had leapt up, but only at that point. Ward agreed that he would not attempt any more impromptu exposures and this seemed to please all as the séance continued, much as it had done before.

A second séance was performed that evening and it was similar in broad respects to the afternoon version. Some new effects were witnessed such as Mr Fay's coat being removed whilst he was still secure in bindings. At this one audience member, a Mr Reed, asked if his coat could be placed on Mr Fay and it did indeed happen.

All members were happy that both séances were genuine and that they had been present for the manifestation of spirits of the dead; all members that is apart from the match-wielding Mr Ward.

On 4 November the Davenports performed another séance. This one was in the Long Room of the Queen's Head on Pilgrim Street (now known as Alderman Fenwick's House). As a brief aside, in the 1990s this house was undergoing renovations and, as befits a house of this antiquity, when it was ripped asunder archaeologists were invited in. Under the hearth of one of the fireplaces they found the remains of a mummified cat. This had evidently been placed there to keep the house safe from evil spirits, a common enough practice in times past when important buildings had human remains built in – for example Hadrian's Wall has been found to have human blood mixed in with some of the mortar. But back to the séance.

The events of this evening were similar to the previous séances described above, but they were open to anyone who could afford the one guinea admission fee. The next evening, 5 November, the Davenports were performing again. This time their venue was a lecture room in Nelson Street and this was to be a séance for the cheaper end of the market. The top price tickets were 10s 6d and the cheap seats were 5s. They still managed to pull in an audience of some 300. One of these audience members, Richard Lowry, recorded in his diary that the audience felt disappointed and swindled. Exactly why they had this reaction to the show is not related and it was definitely not felt by all, as a letter to the *Newcastle Chronicle* shows:

I have only this remark to make. I have seen nearly all the greatest conjurors of the present day. I have been behind the scenes, and assisted in making the necessary preparations for a wizard's entertainment. I have seen both M. Tolmaque and Mr Redmond do their rope trick, and I know how it is done. I can honestly declare that what the Davenports do as far surpasses Anderson, Tolmaque, and Redmond, as these gentlemen can surpass such a clumsy amateur as I am. I am totally at a loss to account for the Davenports' feats by any known principle of legerdemain. If what they do is conjuring, all I can say about it is that it is the cleverest conjuring I ever saw or heard of.

Spiritualism and séances were soon to become the flavour of the month in Newcastle as in 1872 the Newcastle Society for the Investigation of Spiritualism was formed. Many of the members of this society soon discovered that they themselves were mediums. And in 1873 the most gifted of these mediums were found to be seventeen-year-old Annie Fairlamb and eighteen-year-old Miss C.E. Wood, the latter of whom had a father who was greatly interested in spiritualism. It was felt that both mediums were so gifted that they were actually employed by the society specifically for the purposes of investigation. Some of the manifestations and phenomena they were capable of producing were similar to those of the Davenport brothers some nine years previously. Both mediums were felt to be so gifted that they were loaned out to other psychical researchers, including some of the leading lights of the Society for Psychical Research – Frederic Myers and Edmund Gurney. These two gentlemen attended one of the séances in Newcastle and whilst there they witnessed a dematerialisation. Miss Wood had a spirit guide named Pocky, (also known as Pocha or Pocka) who they saw position herself in front of Miss Woods spirit cabinet and they then watched as the spirit guide dematerialised herself, sinking away into a slight white mark on the ground in about half a minute. The mark soon disappeared. Both mediums were taken to London for various shows where they performed and where they often materialised the spirit of a dead relative of one of the sitters. It must be reported that unconnected observers commented on the similarity of each spirit manifestation, whereas the relatives were impressed by how much they looked like the dearly departed.

In test conditions in a London séance of 1875 the two young ladies were placed in a locked wire cage within their cabinet. They themselves were then tied around the waist and ankles by long leather straps which were then fastened to marble pillars. Both mediums were able to call forth their spirits as normal.

Fairlamb was initially paid a princely sum of two guineas per week for use of her talents. This was subsequently changed to a requirement for one séance per week for members who would pay 6d each. As part of the deal Fairlamb had use of the society's rooms on Friday evening and

Sunday morning and she could use these times for private sessions for which she charged 1*s* per head. One official of the society reported that at her height Fairlamb had delivered 141 séances over a six-month period. For this she received the veritable king's ransom of nearly £70, and this was at a time where an experienced parlour maid would have commanded only £20 per annum. Naturally the two girls started out as friends, but the money situation soon drove a rift between them. In 1876 Miss Wood withdrew her services from the society and the following year (after many arguments and disagreements with council members of the society) Annie Fairlamb also walked out. The society was not impressed by this turn of events and they published details of the financial arrangement previously mentioned. The society also sought to point out that Annie had married a member of the group, James Barr Mellon, who had an iron grip on her affairs. It was felt that Mellon was in it for the money. Annie continued her mediumistic work for a number of years after her marriage. One society member, William Armstrong, who stood by Annie, felt that she had been hard done by the society and he particularly mentioned the insults and annoyance that the mediums had to put up with from the alcoholic elements of the audience.

During the later years of the 1870s Miss Wood started to run into problems: at times she felt unable to perform (most noticeably when her helpers were not present) and at other times the crowd were not happy with what they received. One séance was described as being overtaken by evil spirits which displayed 'the most stubborn aspect of human nature… combined with low, reckless manners.' It is felt that this was spiritualist polite speak for the use of unacceptable language and lewd or violent behaviour. Eventually Miss Wood left Newcastle and continued performing séances throughout the UK and she also took to finding more spirits at the bottom of a bottle. Fortunately she came to her senses and she soon returned to a more stable existence in Newcastle and her star began to ascend again… until 1882. In this year *Light* (the newspaper of the London Spiritualist Alliance) reported that during a Newcastle séance the spirit of Pocky had been seized (normally an act which is said to bring great danger to the medium). The seized spirit was found to be Miss Wood on her knees, partially undressed and frantically trying to hide large quantities of muslin. Subsequent letters in *Light* offered explanations including possession by evil spirits, unconscious fraud, the spirit merging with Miss Wood exactly as she was molested and finally the fake items were thrown onto the floor by the attempted exposer himself.

One of Miss Wood's normal private séances was described by T.B. Barkas in *Medium and Daybreak*:

I have seen, through the mediumship of Miss Wood, in a private house, living forms walk from the curtained recess, which it was utterly impossible for her to simulate. I have seen children, women and men of various ages, walk forth under her mediumship. I have seen a materialised form and the medium at the same time. I have had through her mediumship a childlike form standing beside me for about half an hour together; the child has placed its arms around my neck and permitted me at the same time to place my arm around her neck, and has laid its cheek against mine, breathed upon my face, and, in fact caressed me precisely as a child would do to its parent or guardian. This was not in darkness but in light, and in the presence of professors and fellows of one of the leading universities in the Kingdom. I have, under these conditions, and after having handled the psychic form seen it gradually vanish or dematerialise and become invisible in the middle of the room.

A report of Miss Woods' spirit guide leaving physical evidence comes to us from Alfred Smedley, writing in 1900. The lapse between events and the appearance of his text may explain the new name for Miss Wood's spirit guide. Smedley starts by telling us that the medium was enclosed in a wire cage and, whilst encumbered, her spirit Bennie dipped his foot into a hot dish of paraffin and then cold water. He then crossed his legs, tapped his left foot and slowly dematerialised his leg. As the paraffin shoe freed itself Bennie handed it to a witness. Another spirit did the same, this time the spirit was Maggie, the deceased sister of the medium. Upon comparing the feet to those of the medium there was quite clearly a size disparity.

The above are just some examples of some of the many Victorian-era séances which took place in any cosmopolitan city throughout the Empire, with no differences in the reported events, merely in the persons involved.

MODERN-DAY SÉANCES

Séances have continued throughout the world since the mid-nineteenth century but now at the start of the twenty-first century they have had something of a resurgence. This resurgence is down to the popularity of ghost hunting as a pastime. And this in turn is down to the popularity of such television programmes as *Most Haunted*, *Ghost Hunters* and *TAPS*. Séances are now an integral part of many on-screen ghost hunts, and anyone participating in real life wants the experience to be as close to the television situation as possible. There are now a large number of dedicated ghost hunting teams throughout the world, and Newcastle is no exception. One Newcastle group is Otherworld North East and since their inception under the auspices of Tony Liddell in 2003 they have carried out a large number of Newcastle-based investigations. In common with most other groups they do travel and their investigations are not limited to one city. However, it is Newcastle we are interested in and one Newcastle investigation was carried out in 2003 at the Literary and Philosophical Society (the Lit and Phil) of 23 Westgate Road.

The Lit and Phil was founded in 1793 originally as a 'conversation club' with an annual membership fee of one guinea. Religion and politics were banned subjects for discussion and the original library represented this fact as these topics were excluded from their collection. A ground-breaking society, the Lit and Phil admitted their first women members in 1804 and their lecture theatre was the first public room to be lit by an electric light in 1880, courtesy of the Sunderland inventor of the electric light bulb Joseph Swan. As an aside, Swan invented the electric light bulb before American inventor Thomas Alva Edison and Swan patented it in the UK, but not America. Edison modified Swan's original designs slightly and took out a patent in the USA and then waged a rather impressive publicity campaign to convince people that he had invented it himself. Swan was not too interested in making money and was happy to let Edison have the US patent.

The current building occupied by the Lit and Phil had its foundation stone laid in 1822 by the Duke of Sussex. There was then a celebratory meal which included thirty-five toasts and fifty-three speeches. It's no wonder the building wasn't completed until 1825! The society now houses some 150,000 books and thankfully they have discarded the nineteenth-century practice of cataloguing and storing them based on size.

Literary and Philosophical Society library, location of Otherworld North East ghost hunts.

The Other World North East investigation was carried out on the night of 12 December 2003 and this is the first recorded paranormal investigation to take place in the Lit and Phil. All told there were eleven people involved in the investigation and there was a caretaker present in the building the whole time it was under investigation. Unlike the nineteenth century, today a spiritual investigation and séance is not complete without the sort of gadgets that would make James Bond proud. Laser temperature probes, voice-activated digital recorders, EMF meters, motion sensors, night-vision cameras, digital and film cameras, computers and a few non high-tech items for good measure are the basics. Some items used in this type of investigation have no real reason to be there other than they are used on the television investigations – mind you, better safe than sorry.

Preparation is vital in a venture such as this, so records were scoured for previous ghost reports. Organiser Tony Liddell located several, including a named ghost, that of T.H. Marr (subsequent spirit communication claimed that he was an ex-librarian). Reports of shadowy figures were also found as were the sounds of phantom pages turning. As part of the preparatory work the night before the investigation a baseline check was made. Temperatures and EMF levels were recorded to compare against figures collected later. On the actual night of the investigation the first thing to take place was a walk around the building with the group's mediums. During this, two names were picked up: those of James Scott and the Revd Turner, the latter was associated with the term 'founder'.

During the course of the investigation proper each room was visited several times by different groups and over the night some temperature fluctuations were recorded with values moving rapidly between 18.9°C and 26°C. A few members of the team reported feelings of being watched. One of the mediums was able to get a message from a spirit claiming that they were happy in the Lit and Phil. At various parts of the building lights were glimpsed and again vague feelings were reported with the most concrete being one team member reporting a feeling of their trouser leg being pulled. Camera batteries were reported to be draining at an accelerated rate and at 4.30 a.m. some of the most dramatic events of the evening were recorded in the library. Temperatures were rapidly fluctuating and some torch and camera batteries gave out at the same time. Then the medium reported the presence of T.H. Marr in the room with them and that he was trying to influence or enter one of them, at this point organiser Tony Liddell reported a pressure on his neck and shoulders as if someone were pressing down on him. Tony then felt sick and other members of the group reported that their legs had gone weak. It was then reported that Marr did not actually mean any harm, but, as he lacked the strength to materialise physically, he was just trying to let everyone know that he was there in the only way that he could. Surely a few raps of the wall in the style of the Fox sisters, communications would have done the job just as well?

In the Boiler room of the building one of the mediums had sensed two spirits: Revd Turner and Henry Stapleton, the latter of whom had an air of mischief about him. The same medium then picked up on a spirit called Thomas who was a chemist who had followed them from the library out of sheer curiosity. When conducting some dowsing with a pendulum in the boiler room, a contact was made who claimed to be male. After repeating this information the pendulum then stopped dead. When the dowsing restarted, it began with the same questions but this time the responses were clear that the entity was female. When asked to spell out her name, the name Aimie was given and afterwards the pendulum stopped dead and further dowsing was judged not possible. Other spirits picked up by mediums within the Lit and Phil included Charles Bigg, Revd John H. Bruce, Hugh (who refused to give his surname), Elizabeth Spencer-Watson and someone named Swan who seemed to have a connection with the grandfather of Spencer-Watson. Swan seemed to be connected to the seventeenth century and Spencer-Watson to the nineteenth. Another seventeenth-century connection was made with a spirit who had visited China and learnt Chinese. At this point Kay Easson, the librarian at the Lit and Phil who was accompanying the investigation, said that she knew of a man named Robert Morris from the seventeenth century who had connections with both the building and China.

The reading room of the Lit and Phil revealed two spirits, one a woman, Ruth D. She was felt to be a campaigner for women's rights and there was also a male spirit present called Richard Welford. It was here that phantom page turnings would often be heard. There was also communication with the spirit of a child of eight to ten years old called Emily Braithwait in the reading room.

In the main library a veritable plethora of reverends were encountered: first was a pompous spirit called the Revd William Turner and then a rather indistinguishable name which was either the Revd Bells or Belzer. There was a suggestion from the medium that objects would be frequently moved around in this room, this was not something that Kay had heard. Continued presence in this room revealed a female spirit with the surname Dodds, who was then revealed to be the spirit Ruth D. previously encountered in the Reading Room. The curious chemist Thomas was revealed to be still following the group around with interest. A subsequent visit

Literary and Philosophical Society Reading Room where phantom page turnings can be heard.

to the library revealed Thomas Brockett who was nervous of the group. It seems unlikely that this is the chemist Thomas, but it is of course possible. Thomas, it appeared, was looking for his favourite book *Chevney Papers*. The medium asked Thomas to guide his torch to the book on the shelves. The torch moved over the shelves for some thirty seconds before settling on a book, and when the spot was examined it was found to be the resting site of the correct book published in 1903 and being taken from the papers of Thomas Creary MP. Another spirit that was picked up was that of a child named Katie Hewitt who was the same age as Emily Braithwait. The library visit yielded the sound of footsteps and people having the feeling they were being prodded in the back. A photograph taken at this time yielded an orb: one of the few events captured on camera that night.

The Ladies Room of the Lit and Phil yielded the presence of a single spirit from 1555, which claimed to be forty-four years old. A long conversation via the pendulum yielded extra details, she was (reasonably) happily married to a wealthy but unintelligent husband and she had two children by him. It appeared that when alive the spirit worked in the area and after confirming that she was happy for the investigators to remain she said that her name was Ruth Dodds. It should be pointed out that the main library information about Ruth Dodds was reported at a separate time by a different medium.

Literary and Philosophical Society Committee Room – haunted by the ghost of a witchfinder.

The Committee Room appeared to contain a negative presence, a spirit that was not connected with the building but that was in fact connected to witchcraft. It was felt that this spirit was a witchfinder and that they had burned 210 people. This was felt to be a strong spirit capable of moving things around and dating from the early-sixteenth century. It must be pointed out that in England the burning of a witch was actually a rare occurrence. Of all people accused of witchcraft, fully three-quarters were found not guilty. Of the remainder only a small number were put to death and the majority of these were executed by hanging. The medium felt unwell and requested to leave the room and later that night two members of the group heard a loud male groan in the Committee Room.

The investigations were carried out by four groups which visited locations at different times. Charles Bigg(e) was picked up here again by a different group and this time it was felt that he was the Sheriff of either Newcastle or Gateshead after 1740. One member of the group felt as if a pressure was building up on them and then another felt a developing toothache. There was also a feeling of a childlike presence hiding under the table in the Committee Room. Another group entered the room and commenced dowsing, they found the spirit of a male who was unhappy with the groups being present; this spirit appeared to be from the thirteenth century. At this point the pendulum was spinning constantly and refusing to stop. When questioning could be resumed they tried to pin down a year; the spirit was asked if it was from 1300–1350, the pendulum spun to indicate 'no', then the question was asked for 1350–1400 to which the pendulum responded 'yes'. A strange response given that the spirit had previously claimed to be from the thirteenth century! Further questioning revealed the spirit to be Scottish with a job which involved violence, although they enjoyed it. The medium had obviously come to a conclusion about who they thought they were communicating with and they asked if our Scottish friend liked witches, to which the answer was 'no'. At this point one of the investigators felt warm on one side of his body and cold on the other and when the spirit was asked if it was him making this happen, to which the reply was 'yes'. Shortly after this the evening drew to an end.

After the session was over the next piece of work was to chase the names and references up – were they real and verifiable? Had any of the events any historical basis or was it all impossible to prove? From the reports of the medium and dowsing with the pendulum there were a total of seventeen specific names. One identifiable name was Richard Welford, a former noteworthy gentleman of Newcastle, his bust is on the stairs at the Lit and Phil and the investigators would have passed it a number of times during the night and walkthrough. The Revd William Turner was one of the founders of the Society and again a bust and a portrait are on display in the entrance area of the Society. T.H. Marr is identified only in a book of ghost stories, where he is listed as a sub-librarian in the Society. For the name of Armstrong things are a bit more difficult as it is a common local name. Charles Bigg was the High Sheriff of Northumberland and one of the purchasers of the land on which the Society is built. Elizabeth Spencer-Watson was president of a large number of organisations within Newcastle and very active in each. Swan, it has been suggested by some, could possibly be Joseph Swan, a Pharmacist, chemist

Literary and Philosophical Society entrance stairway with portraits and bust of some of the spirits sensed by mediums.

and electrical engineer and inventor of the electric light bulb (although he was alive from 1828–1924 and not in the seventeenth century) and finally Ruth Dodds, who was an author and local Labour party councillor.

All told, the conclusions of the investigate team were that the area is psychically very active but that nothing capable of actual harm is present. Otherworld North East were pleased with the whole process and they recommended further investigations be carried out at a future date. Other World North East still continue their investigations, but they no longer rely on the input of mediums as a regular source of information.

Two very different séances carried out for different audiences nearly 150 years apart. But one thing is for sure: the desire to communicate with spirits is still as strong as ever, after all, a piece of definite proof for an existence after this one would be one of the most earth shattering pieces of information we could ever find.

SHE DIDN'T SEE THIS ONE COMING …

But just in case you think everything is well in the world of the Newcastle medium we have the following cautionary tale from October 2008 of the medium who was too good …

The story starts at the Heaton and Byker Spiritualist Church where Amanda Molloy has been a regular attendee since she was fourteen in 1984. As part of the church's services they hold open circle events – readings where a medium transmits information from the other side. These open circles are for other mediums and members of the public to attend, in other words people who are not necessarily spiritualists (spiritualism in this sense being a religion rather than just a general belief in life after death). Eventually Amanda started to give readings herself at these weekly sessions and as she puts it, 'I will get people coming through who have taken their own life, been murdered or died tragically and I get up and say exactly what's being said. I say it as I hear it and it's accurate.' The problem arose when Amanda gave a reading to a member of the audience and in it she described with great detail how her daughter had been murdered. The woman, on hearing these details, was so shocked that she ran out of the meeting. Amanda Molloy then claims, 'The lady who runs the church told me I couldn't say murdered and I shouldn't have walked down the aisle to speak to the woman.' The unnamed woman in charge then alleged that there had been complaints and that Amanda was giving out too much personal information. Amanda was then given a letter from the secretary of the church saying she had broken the rules and had spoken of confidential matters. Amanda's take on all of this is that, 'It's jealousy … I think its ridiculous being told off for being spot on. I won't be going back.' One thing is for sure: whatever Amanda's powers, she didn't see this one coming!

DESPERATE FOR THE PHOTOGRAPHS

In the latter part of the nineteenth century a Mr Dickinson had a photographer's shop on Grainger Street and the following story of an event that occurred at his shop is related in *Real Ghost Stories* by W.T. Stead, published in 1891. On the morning of Saturday 3 January, 1890, a Mr Thompson called to collect his previously sat for photographs. Mr Thompson did not have his receipt but they were able to work out that his photographs had been taken on

6 December. Mr Thompson was told that the photographs were not yet ready and could he call again later? Mr Thompson, with a measure of displeasure, replied that he could not. He had been travelling all night and he was already very tired. At this point he left the photographer's studio. Mr Dickinson remembers thinking at the time that the gentleman looked very ill and he determined to complete the order as soon as possible. On 9 January Mr Thompson's father arrived to collect the photographs. Mr Dickinson enquired after his son, to be told that he had died on the previous Saturday, the 3 January. In fact he had died at 2.30 p.m. and for the previous part of the day he had been unconscious. Before passing out the night before, he had been delirious and had called out many times for his portrait pictures.

There are many reports in the literature of a category of ghost called a crisis apparition. These appear, usually at the time of death, to carry out a task that had been preying on the mind of the recently deceased or to say their farewells to a friend or family member. Is it possible that the portrait was so important to young Mr Thompson that not even death could stop him collecting it?

Stead's book recounting the tale was felt to be so scary that the front part of it contained a warning:

Before reading the contents of this Christmas number, please note:

1. That the narratives printed in these pages had better not be read by any one of tender years, of morbid excitability, or of excessively nervous temperament.

2. That the latest students of the subject concur in the solemn warning addressed in the Sacred Writings to those who have dealings with familiar spirits, or who expose themselves to the horrible consequences of possession.

3. That as the latent possibilities of our complex personality are so imperfectly understood, all experimenting in hypnotism, spiritualism, etc., excepting in the most careful and reverent spirit, by the most level headed persons had much better be avoided.

This caution is printed here at the suggestion of **Catholics**, **Theosophists**, and **Spiritualists**, who declare themselves to be profoundly convinced of its **necessity**. [Emphasis in original.]

MODERN GHOST HUNTERS

One of the many Newcastle-based ghost groups is the Newcastle Paranormal Investigation Group. Founded by John Stock in 2007, it has its origins in an event Stock witnessed at Jarrow Cemetery. As a seventeen-year-old, Stock and two friends had been walking home after a night out when they spotted a figure in white. After initially ignoring it they realised the figure was now starting to move towards them, Stock thought this strange as. 'There were three of us and we were all into heavy metal at the time and had long hair ... Then the figure started sprinting towards us, it was completely white from head to toe and looked like a female. We ran off. I can't think it could have been anything other than a ghost.' It would appear that this group is now defunct. One group that is still active and is recruiting members is Paranormal UK. Similarly, Other World North East are still very active, but unfortunately the 1872 Newcastle Society for the Investigation of Spiritualism has gone away. In 2009 the Newcastle Fortean

Modern view of the castle from the railway station, showing extensive renovations being undertaken.

The Castle Keep.

Society started up and Alone in the Dark Entertainment run a series of events from walks to training sessions and investigations. A number of one-off events take place as well, usually in aid of charity, and these are usually well publicised in advance.

In 2005 UK Living TV's *Most Haunted* came to investigate Newcastle with medium Derek Acorah. The vigil was centred on the Castle Keep (Castle Garth to give it its proper name) and the show was first broadcast on 8 November 2005. Previous reports were discussed. These included people being slapped by unseen hands, sightings of a figure carrying some sort of backpack, footsteps heard, mists seen, hammering on doors, lights following people around, figures being sensed, dragging of metal on stone and finally a sound of chanting that had been recorded in the chapel. The two psychics of the show both identified a female spirit associated with flowers, they were not sure if she was holding onto them or handing them out. A number of different noises were heard, including a brass band even though there was no evidence of one in the vicinity. Rooms that were used by the crew had furniture moved whilst no one was present and finally Karl Beattie (husband of the presenter Yvette Fielding and executive producer and director) was reciting the Lord's Prayer during a solo vigil and twice he was interrupted by heavy knocking.

Since the broadcast of *Most Haunted* most of these ghosts have again been reported in the Castle Keep.

five

WITCHCRAFT, MAGIC AND LUCK

WITCHCRAFT TRIALS

One shameful chapter in the history of Europe was felt strongly in Newcastle, although not as extensively as in some other areas.

Nowadays the mere mention of a witch conjures up the Halloween version, a wizened old crone riding on a broomstick. But in reality, in the Middle Ages and Early Modern period anyone could be a witch and for a trial to be initiated all someone had to do was to accuse a person of being one. Mere trifles such as evidence were irrelevant at the start of the case and as you will see evidence was largely irrelevant throughout the whole proceedings. Unlike other acts of law a witch was assumed guilty until proven innocent and the trial could be started on an anonymous, unsupported accusation.

One example of a typical outbreak of witchcraft hysteria took place on 26 March 1649 when thirty suspected witches were put on trial. Of these twenty seven were found guilty. Fourteen were subsequently executed on the Town Moor. The places of execution are still extant today although the exact spots are lost to the mists of time. The guilt of the witches had been confirmed by a Scottish witch finder whose name is lost to posterity (Alone in the Dark Tours believe he was called Cuthbert Nicholson but Pamela Anderson in *Dark Tales of Old Newcastle* claims it was John Kincaid). A witch finder was a person trained in the detection of practitioners of the dark arts. A witch finder was paid a fee for every witch they successfully found. The more witches the more money. Not the fairest of wage settlements, particularly when a guilty verdict, and therefore a fee, often meant death or imprisonment of a person. Newcastle Council asked for people to report all witches and the thirty previously mentioned were duly reported.

The supposed witches were stripped to the waist and the witch finder would then prick them with a pin. If they bled they were innocent (until the next time someone accused them and they were tested again), and if they did not bleed they were judged to be guilty and the witch finder would be paid his *20s* per witch. Naturally this whole procedure was carried out in the Town Hall watched by the relevant judges and any members of the public who wished to attend. In the days before television, for some, this was the ultimate night out. The Town Hall would be packed full whilst each woman was stripped to the waist in turn.

Suitably exposed to one and all, along with fear and panic, there would also be embarrassment. When embarrassed we tend to blush, even in such a horrific situation as described. When we blush the blood rushes to our faces temporarily leaving some areas pale and bereft of blood. The practical upshot of this is, if you time it right, it's possible to embarrass someone and stick them with a pin and for a few seconds there is little chance of bleeding occurring. This technique is an instant way of earning 20s and condemning a random person to death for witchcraft. If the relevant witch finder was indeed Nicholson it is somewhat fitting to note that he was executed in Scotland for trickery but not before, by his own admission, sending 220 women to their deaths (Anderson records the same fate for Kincaid). The witches found guilty were hanged on the Town Moor on 21 August 1650. The bodies were buried in St Andrew's churchyard, indeed the parish register records 6d paid 'for a grave for a witch.' At the time iron rivets were placed in the knees of an executed witch to make sure she would not rise and walk again. Burning at the stake was actually an uncommon form of execution for witches, particularly in the Newcastle area.

Another technique for testing if a person was a witch relied on the fact that many blamed witches for diseases that were visited upon them. The witch believed to have cast the enchantment was taken and blood was drawn from her forehead and this was then applied to the victim and this was supposed to cure them. A neat side effect of this cure was that if the victim did indeed get better than this proved that the person who had been bled was indeed a witch.

But these are not the earliest stories of witchcraft from the region. For that we have to go back to the thirteenth century! And also a little bit outside Newcastle to Kerneslawe, Northumberland, remember that at this time Newcastle was part of that county. A man by the name of John claimed he was attacked in his house by a witch and in defending himself he killed her. Temporarily driven insane by this action John ran away but, on regaining his senses, he took refuge with the local bishop. John did not need to worry. His actions of killing a witch were not looked on as a serious crime. He merely paid a fine and the body of his victim was burnt by the local authorities – just in case! Of course those with a less than charitable view of the events could say that by describing his victim as a witch he managed to save himself from a death sentence for murder!

And not all who were suspected of witchcraft were burnt (dead or alive) at the stake. For example if someone was regarded as a healer who used herbs, a practice frowned upon by the church, but often used by locals, and they managed to upset someone in power then action would have to be seen to be taken. This usually took the form of some sort of public humiliation; this could include public confession (often in church) or time in the stocks; neither perhaps pleasant, but a lot better than drowning or burning, which was the fate of many witches.

One case of a herbalist healer suffering various indignities is that of Janet Pereson of Wallsend. In 1570 she attempted to treat a young boy who was troubled by fairies. She bade him to wash in some water (an unusual practice for the sixteenth century), wet a shirt with the water and then hang it on a hedge. In the morning the shirt would be gone and the fairies would no longer trouble the child. Unfortunately there were no shirt thieves aboat that night so the shirt remained where it was. As the cure had manifestly failed, Pereson was dutifully reported to the church authorities.

Another who was reported as a witch after a failed cure was a midwife named Mrs Pepper who, in 1662, fell foul of the authorities. A pit worker named Robert Pyle was suffering from head pains and stomach discomfort and as a last resort he consulted Mrs Pepper. Mrs Pepper sprinkled water on his face and gave him the bottle telling him to apply it as necessary. She also

The town moor where witches were executed.

St Andrew's churchyard, where *6d* would buy you a grave for a witch complete with iron rivets in their knees to stop them walking about after their death.

treated him with a silver crucifix and made him breathe in the breath of two children which would, apparently, suck out the evil spirits causing his maladies. The cure failed and Mrs Pepper was accused of witchcraft. Cue the ritual humiliation. Presumably if Pyle had been cured he would have paid his dues and not said a peep about Mrs Pepper's unusual techniques.

Two more healers falling foul of witchcraft laws were Jane Watson and Anne Mennin. It was said, in 1661, that two children of Katherine Cudworth (wife of a Newcastle woollen draper) fell ill and that the two healers tormented them at night. On one occasion the two children were suffering fits and one cried out that she could see Watson and that she had brought her an apple. One of the servants of the house confirmed the story saying that she too could see Jane Watson, apparently going so far as to describe what she was wearing. The shade of Watson was then reported to have disappeared under the bed. One gentleman present had the great presence of mind to thrust his sword under the bed. As he did this there was heard a pig-like noise, which was followed by a flash of fire and then a round ball of fire flew up the chimney (ball lightning or a witch fleeing?). More spookily, a half eaten apple was found at the head of the bed. Both healers were tried as witches, Jane Watson was acquitted but bizarrely Mennin, who it appeared took no part in the supposed proceedings, was found guilty. Mennin had been found guilty of witchcraft on three occasions previously and her husband was less than pleased, but he did see a way out of the situation, which would leave him free to continue his assignations with their housekeeper. He sent bread laced with arsenic to his wife in prison. The bread was eaten, Anne died. During the autopsy two surgeons found traces of arsenic in her stomach and traces were also found in the remnants of the bread; an early form of *CSI*-style justice.

Of course some believe that even reading tea leaves, the tarot cards or any form of divination is the act of the dark arts and witchcraft. Well I can confirm that a genuine gypsy is flaunting the past record of Newcastle and these sorts of matters. Most weekends Gypsy Kathleen or Angeline Lee (they share the caravan) can be found complete with caravan at the top of Bigg Market for those who fancy knowing what the future holds. But the gypsy Lee should be careful, for in 1758 a group of fortune tellers had some bad fortune in Newcastle. Four women were pilloried – a kind of standing up stocks which added a new level of discomfort to the whole process: whilst in the pillory rotten fruit can be thrown at the victim, exactly as seen in the movies. The sentence was often one of repeated exposure to the pillory over a long period of time rather than a single session. One of the women so pilloried was Susanna Fleming, an eighty-year-old. She was sentenced to be pilloried for one hour every quarter for a year. Naturally the whole process was worse for her than her younger colleagues and she eventually had to be removed from the stocks as her life was in peril – the pain was too much for her and she started to collapse so that the weight of her whole body was put onto her neck and she started to choke. A member of the public who had been observing the proceedings realised the danger she was in and rescued her from potential suffocation.

In 1755 another fortune teller fell foul of the laws – James Lawson was ultimately made to stand pilloried on four separate occasions for 'pretending to tell fortunes and find lost goods.'

CHARMS

In 1670 Peter Banks had himself a nice little earner according to author Jo Bath. Banks sold leases for 20s and during the year that the lease ran for, the customer could not die. As can be

Gypsy caravan in Bigg market, an opportunity for your fortune to be told.

imagined this was a popular thing to buy. The lease was a charm written on a piece of paper. Bath reports that the charm read, 'I charge you and all of you in the high sword name to assist and bless — belonging to such and such a ship… from all rocks and sands, storms and tempests, thereunto belonging for this year.' Although written for sailors others bought into the lease idea and there is one instance of a woman finding her husband's lease and burning it. Not because she wanted him to die, but merely as she felt he was being foolish for wasting his money on such a thing. Banks was not happy with this and predicted (or cursed) that she would never be worth more than the smallest amount of money. And sure enough the family rapidly lost all their wealth. A bit unfortunate for the poor husband! Banks was also able to command evil spirits and he would use this power to heal the sick as well as to guarantee life for longer than a year. Banks also sold leases to make husbands kind and loving. Banks was eventually taken to court for 'arts magic called charms and spells, and assuming upon himself by the same art to procure safety at sea.' It is not clear whether the complainant was the relative of someone who had died whilst owning a lease or a husband who did not want to be kind and loving. Whichever it was Banks was eventually acquitted, but surely afterwards he must have been more careful in his affairs.

In the eighteenth century Sir Francis Deleval told a tale of an ancestor of his who had dealings with a witch. The unnamed ancestor investigated a Wallsend church that was lit up at night. And when he crept inside he found to his surprise that there was a coven of witches in the church. The inquisitive ancestor of Deleval found that the witches appeared to be hacking up the corpse of a woman, presumably for use in charms. Deleval's ancestor burst into the church and the witches fled, but he was able to catch hold of and retain one. In common with some of the more unlucky witches she was condemned to be burnt to death on Seaton Sands. As she was being taken to the stake she begged to be given two wooden plates, a request which was granted. As the fire was lit she put the plates beneath her feet and muttered a spell under her breath. As she finished her incantation she started to rise up above the flames. However, one of the plates had been dipped in water before being given to the witch, and it gave way, plunging her back into the flames.

BLACK JACKY JOHNSON

In the early years of the nineteenth century Black Jacky Johnson of Dog Bank (a self-proclaimed professor of the Black Arts) owned a magic mirror. This mirror was supposedly made following instructions laid down by the Greek Magus (an ancient magician or priest) Cornelius Agrippa. This mirror was a rather useful and popular invention and it was responsible for a multitude of tasks: it could find the identity of a husband for a woman, tell the hidden meaning behind dreams and as an encore it could locate stolen goods. So powerful was the reputation of Black Jacky Johnson that some thieves were known to return their ill-gotten gains purely on the strength of a victim going to him.

The Corporation of Newcastle were not in favour of the actions of Johnson and eventually drove him out of Dog Bank, and he set up home in a separate area of Newcastle, Byker Bar. In 1837 Johnson died whilst telling the fortune of someone with tarot cards. As he had no family to tell of Johnson felt it would be a good idea to leave all his spell books to the people of Newcastle. Some of the spells seem to be rather useful indeed. One splendid example of one of the spells of Black Jacky Johnson is one to render a person invisible. The person wishing to make themselves invisible needs to get a pure black cat, one with not even a single white hair on its body. It must be boiled for three hours on a Sunday during a religious service. Once this has been carried out the heart of the cat is removed and dried in an oven that has never been used. Once the heart has been dried it is reduced to a powder and over seven nights the powder is concealed around a churchyard at midnight. On the final night as you are walking to the churchyard you will meet someone else who will walk with you to the churchyard, upon arrival at the churchyard half of the remaining powder must be given to the stranger. Once all this has been done whenever you carry any of the powder around with you then you will be invisible!

No desire to become invisible? Perhaps you suffer from acne — well fear not, for Johnson had a cure for that in his books. You must collect one pebble from the beach for every spot of acne. The pebbles must be placed in a cloth bag and left at a crossroads. When a nosy passer-by sees the bag and picks it up the acne is transferred to them. The acne cure is a lot easier to use than the secret of invisibility!

When Johnson was still alive he used to meet with fellow witches and wizards at Tambourine House in the Sandgate, a popular spot for local covens to gather, apparently. As well as the house of choice for witches this was also the local house of ill repute, it is possible that one of these reputations was artificially gained to keep inquisitive children away. The building was eventually demolished in the 1800s although it stood at the west end of St Annes Street.

The Sandgate witches were serious about what they did and one night they attempted an Esbat — a special ceremony to call up the Devil. The Devil duly appeared and he did so in the form of a very ordinary looking man. This man gorged himself on all of the food available and in doing so he ignored the orgies taking place around him. Just in case you were worried that this was merely a local who had wandered in and taken advantage of the situation, an event happened at 1 a.m. to dispel this idea. At the end of his appearance the devil strode to the centre of the room, stood stock still, he then shot off like a rocket through the roof, whether the roof was damaged in the process or whether he transported himself through it is not recorded.

THE PLAGUE

Newcastle has not always been a lucky place. In 1636 plague hit the city hard. But Geordies being what they were even then, they got on with their lives as best as they could. Then in 1646 Newcastle was hit by the plague again. But the Corporation of Newcastle – essentially the great and the good of the city – had a plan. They sent to Scotland for a device which they knew would save their city. They were after the Lee Penny, a penny which when immersed in water would imbue the water with power – the power of immunity for life from the plague. The Lee family, as can be imagined, made good money from hiring out this amulet! And if anyone doubted its veracity the Lee Penny came with appropriate paperwork extolling its virtues: letters from those who had drank and survived whilst others around them dropped like flies. The Corporation tried to buy the Lee Penny and insisted they held onto it whilst negotiations took place. The Lee family were not happy with this and suspected some underhand tactics by the good burgesses of Newcastle. The Lees were able to gain access to the Penny and managed to spirit it back to Scotland. Naturally without the Lee Penny to ward off the plague, many lives were lost in Newcastle. However, there are no records of plague victims haunting any areas of Newcastle.

six

SOMETHING IN THE SKY - UFOs

According to documents recently released from the Ministry of Defence and available for viewing at the National Archives at Kew, London, Newcastle has suffered a recent spate of UFO sightings. For example on 30 June 1987 a security guard in Newcastle had a fifteen to twenty minute long sighting of a multitude of lights. The former member of the military said he watched, 'A large, white light … travelling west to east.' The other five lights travelled in various directions. The weather that night was described as clear with good visibility.

On 6 March 1987 a green object was seen above the skies of Newcastle and this was separately reported by three witnesses. One witness described a pale, bright green object which gave off no sound or smell and it had a steady movement and then it just disappeared. A second witness was able to watch the object from outside his house for several minutes and this witness described it as green and glowing. Both of these Gosforth residents reported their sightings to the police. The third witness was at Longbenton when they sighted a green sphere for five minutes. Also concerned, this individual informed the police.

Gosforth seems to supply rich pickings for the UFO spotter. Richard Dawson reported a UFO sighting on 23 August 2007. The sighting actually took place in November 2003 but it's the nature of many of these things that they're not reported at the time. Dawson and a friend were climbing out of a car in Gosforth when the friend suddenly spotted something in the sky. In Dawson's words, 'I looked and saw the black triangle, which was at about the height of five or six houses, glide over our heads, really smooth – and it was absolutely silent.' The supposed craft came from south-east of Dawson's location, from Jesmond, and flew off in a north-westerly direction, last seen heading towards Broadway West. Dawson reports that it was flying at a speed of 30–40 mph. How he was able to discern this from an object of unknown size at an unknown distance is unclear. Dawson went on to describe the craft as having a dimly glowing red circle on the bottom and he noted the absence of lights on the corners of the craft. Dawson was also certain that the triangle was jet black in colour. Due to Dawson's late reporting he can't remember the exact date, but he is pretty sure it took place between 7 and 8 p.m.

Another 2003 sighting was reported from Gateshead: an anonymous witness stated that they had seen, 'One black orb with five or six tassels underneath it,' and it was heading towards Newcastle. The witness was sufficiently concerned to contact the Ministry of Defence about their sighting. The MOD felt it was of no defence significance – whatever it was – and pursued the matter no further.

Northumbria University, based in Newcastle, has a sociologist who lectures on UFOs and abduction phenomena. This is Lee Barron. Barron is on record when talking to the *Evening Chronicle* as pointing out the similarity of form of television and film aliens and those subsequently reported by the public. Barron says that in the early years simple craft were reported, as featured in programmes such as *The Twilight Zone* and *The Outer Limits*. As time has progressed and film makers' technical ability has improved so has the complexity of the craft seen – think of the craft from *Close Encounters of the Third Kind* and then go back to our anonymous Gateshead witness. Barron also links the appearance of triangular UFOs with the emergence into the skies of the American Stealth craft – such as the F117.

On New Year's Day 1982 Wendy Garrat, a photographer based in Wallsend, saw a flying object ten to fifteen times the size of a star. In March of that year two police officers witnessed a UFO hovering over the Tyne Valley for more than an hour. Even though the sighting lasted such a long time they did not have a camera themselves nor did they think to contact someone who could supply one.

AIRPORT UFOs

October 1985 saw Newcastle Airport apparently buzzed by... something! An air traffic controller (surely an excellent witness for this sort of thing) and his assistant spotted two unknown objects in the sky above the airfield. The two objects had lights, one of which was described as bright and the other dim. Another witness outside the airport also saw the lights, as did a pilot of a light aircraft six miles from the airport. During the latter half of 1987 a customs officer at Newcastle airport spotted a cigar-shaped object, gold and orange in colour, displaying bright lights. The witness was able to watch for two or three minutes and they also reported this sighting to the police. In November 1987 someone was able to record a much longer sighting: some fifteen to twenty minutes of blue and amber lights. 'One object, approximately the size of a helicopter, with blue and amber lights – very bright.' These last two reports are from the vicinity of an airport where you would expect to see things in the sky, but you would also hope that those employed there would be able to recognise a plane when they saw one. There is another airport in the vicinity of Newcastle, RAF Boulmer, and UFOs have been reported from that area too. After a 1987 sighting, the base was contacted to see if they could offer any clue as to the identity of the craft or could they offer any form of corroboration to the sightings? The squadron leader replied in a letter:

We have checked our records for the period April 2 to 22, 1987, and are unable to confirm or deny that your reports of unknown targets originated from aircraft taking part in exercises being carried out at the time ... I can inform you that our day to day practice sorties are carried out over the North Sea and would not normally be visible from the coast ... However, between April 6 and 10, 1987, we were involved in Exercise Mallet Blow and from April 13 to April 15, Exercise Priory took place in a similar area. Both of these events did include a number of low flying target aircraft which would have flown inland from the North Sea toward firing ranges from the Otterburn area ... Unfortunately I am unable to tie any particular aircraft to any given UFO sightings.

The evening of Tuesday 25 October 2000 provided a multiple-witness event which also saw the object being tracked across the North-East. The first report is from Penshaw (some ten miles from Newcastle) where retired prison worker Ron Atwill, whilst walking his dog, saw a 5ft-long grey object. He also described it as being very flat and pear shaped. He also said it looked like a piece of corrugated iron but not corrugated and oblong! What worried Atwill was the fact that the object appeared to be on an exact collision course with a plane coming in to land at Newcastle airport. Atwill witnessed the plane flying towards Newcastle airport from Harrington Colliery Yard. The airport was visible between Penshaw Monument and the Colliery. The plane was quite low as it was coming in to land and as Atwill watched he thought that the grey UFO almost hit it. So worried was Atwill that he contacted the airport. Even though he was seeing it at a distance it was quite distinct and not a mere speck in the sky. Atwill is convinced that he did not see a weather balloon or a model of any sort. Later that day eighteen-year-old Sunderland University trainee teacher Jenny Cook witnessed a 5ft diameter, pear shaped, silver metal object flying over Hendon, Wearside.

One criticism of UFO reports is that astronomers rarely report them. But some amateur astronomers do. In 1980 fifteen-year-old David Wakenshaw was observing the night sky (looking for a planet through his 10 x 50 binoculars); he was looking at a point south of Orion when he saw a light. Being sensible he initially took it for a plane. As he continued observing it he noticed it kept disappearing and reappearing, which he initially took to be due to clouds. Keen to keep watching through his new binoculars, Wakenshaw saw that the object was approaching closer and he was soon able to confirm that it was not a plane that he could recognise. For five minutes he watched the UFO which he later described as grey in colour with a classic two-plates-on-top-of-each-other shape. He could also see some sort of distortion

View from Penshaw towards Newcastle airport, a line of sight along which a UFO was reported.

to the area behind the UFO. Another sighting from a young witness was on the 13 May 2008 by Benny Armstrong: he saw a dark-coloured disc of an approximate diameter of 10ft, it hovered and it had a ring of white light on its edge.

Many witnesses of UFOs are embarrassed over their experience and they do not report them. Many others only report them if assured on anonymity, hence the lack of names or surnames in this section. For example, Wendy in July 2001 saw:

… a huge bright light above the clouds, orange in colour, it lit up a huge area, roofs of houses etc [it] was hovering at first and then moving slowly. I seen the sky light up, at first I thought it was a helicopter with its spotlight on but there was no noise and the colour of the light I seen was an orange/yellow. The light covered too large an area to be a spotlight anyway! As light moved towards me – I moved towards the light, I was fascinated by it! Somewhere down the line I got frightened and ran home. I watched the light from my bedroom window for some time, until it just zoomed away fast. I lost quite a bit of time. I have nightmares. I sometimes wake up with strange red marks and/or scratches with no explanation how or why. I am in constant pain that more or less started overnight. I have a fascination with looking at the sky at night time. I have often found myself sitting outside looking at the night sky as if I'm waiting for something. I feel embarrassed about the whole thing because I can't get my head around it all.

Rather surprisingly UFO groups do not appear to have followed this sighting up, but it does seem to bear many of the hallmarks of what they would regard as a suppressed abduction case, making this the only reported Newcastle alien abduction. Anonymity can make it hard to follow these sightings up but the person to whom it is originally reported has got the person's contact details.

Stephen Appleby saw a modern-style UFO in 2004: a black triangle. At 2 p.m. on 22 August Stephen described seeing a triangle about 6ft tall and 4ft across, like a black shining glass object, it also had blue and red lights at its base. The object was first seen hovering some 6ft above the ground and as Stephen approached it, it would move away from him. Eventually the object shot upwards at a great speed. Stephen does not say how close he ultimately got to the object, but he watched and interacted with it for twenty-five minutes on the Freeman Road. He took a photograph with his camera phone, but he refuses to release it saying he will give it to the correct people when the time comes.

Another triangle had been seen earlier on Christmas day 1999 by Hails Mortimer in Newcastle city centre. For twenty minutes Mortimer watched a triangle floating in the sky, it merely hovered in place until it zoomed off. Throughout the sighting there were no lights visible on the supposed craft.

These are just a small collection of some of the many Newcastle UFO reports. This might look like a lot of reports, but compared to some areas of the country Newcastle is just an 'also ran.'

seven

PARANORMAL MUSHROOMS

FAIRY RINGS

Being a sprawling metropolis of over 250,000 people and containing a large area of concrete, Newcastle does not have much space for the alleged paranormal phenomena of crop circles. A crop circle is a formation or pattern in a field, usually found in corn. These crop circles have been variously ascribed to natural sources, UFOs, 'artists' and two elderly gentlemen called Doug and Dave from Wiltshire. However, there are plenty of spaces left for the folkloric precursor to the crop circle: the Fairy Ring.

A fairy ring is a roughly circular patch of grass which is marked out in one of two main ways. The circle can be marked out either by a dark, lush growth of grass, generally higher than the surrounding grass, or there can be a bare circle of grass. Combinations of the two are also possible with a circle of luxuriant growth and immediately behind it a circle of bare ground.

As the name implies, a Fairy Ring is said to be caused by the action of fairies. For the superstitious amongst you, you may wish to use the phrase Lords and Ladies or the Gentle Folk rather than fairies, as saying the F word may actually encourage them to appear to you. They are not quite the gambolling, happy-go-lucky creatures of some stories. Fairies are a hedonistic race and they enjoy all pleasures available to them, in particular they are fond of dancing. When the night appears, the fairy folk emerge from their realm into ours and they start to dance. As they dance, they move in circles spinning ever faster. Eventually they are rotating at a speed too fast for mortals to comprehend. As the dance finishes the ground shows the wear and tear of many thousands of revolutions of dainty feet. The grass has been worn away to leave a ring of bare earth. And that is how fairy rings can be formed. Many open areas of grassland in Newcastle have fairy rings of varying sizes: the bigger the ring the more fairies taking place in the dance. They can be found from Jesmond Dene to several of the major roads cutting through the city (specifically the grass verges). But if you're not fond of fairies then don't worry, there is an alternative explanation: bare earth fairy rings are produced by amorous hedgehogs running nose to tail in pursuit of each other.

If you're in Newcastle at the end of April there is some good news about fairy rings: if you bathe your face in dew collected from inside a fairy ring on May Day morning then you will

A fairy ring, the location of a previous night's dance.

stay young and beautiful forever. However, beware – if you are standing in the fairy ring when you collect the dew you will be instantly transformed into an aged crone.

On the Town Moor at the north-west end of the city, where cattle can be grazed by those with appropriate rights, there is an explanation for the luxuriant growth form of the fairy ring. During the autumn and winter, when the grass is not all it should be, the cattle can have their feed supplemented by bales of hay. As the cattle are feeding on the hay their heads are all on the hay and to fit as many cattle in as possible they are standing in a loose circle. If their heads are pointing inwards then the opposite end is pointing outwards so the rear end of the cows will also be in a loose circle. As the cows eat the hay their bodies convert the material into, shall we say, natural fertiliser, which is then deposited in a circle from the multitude of cow rear ends. A circle of fertiliser will make the grass grow more luxuriantly in a very localised spot and hence give rise to a ring of good-growth grass.

Yet another explanation is also put down to animal behaviour, but this time it's moles. The moles run in circles under the ground releasing their droppings as they go and again these now hidden droppings act as fertiliser giving the same appearance as the cattle. As to why the moles are running in subterranean circles I'm not quite sure.

In actual fact the real-life solution to how fairy rings are formed is a lot simpler than evoking mythical mischief-makers, but it is none the less just as beautiful: mushrooms. Mushrooms reproduce by means of a special type of seed called a spore. Spores are very similar in size to specks of dust and they can be blown enormous distances, but the important thing is that when they land, if the conditions are right, they will start to grow. Fungal spores do not grow in the same way as plants, which send shoots upwards and roots downwards; what actually happens is a series of cotton wool like threads grow out in a circular pattern all around the spore, these are called mycelia. As time passes the disc of mycelia that has been produced spreads out (this all usually happens underground so it is generally not visible). When the mycelia feed they release chemicals called enzymes into the ground to accelerate the break down of potential foods. The liquid nutrients are then sucked back into the mycelia. Unfortunately fungi are sloppy feeders and not all of the food is taken back. Just as this liquid acts as food for the fungi it will also act as food for growing plants. As the disc of mycelia gets bigger the central part dies so only a narrow, circular strip is alive and, where this extra nutrient is produced, the grass grows more vigorously. The bare patch of grass form of the fairy ring is equally easily explained by the presence of fungi. At the section of the disc where the mycelia are growing most vigorously the mycelia produce a very dense net. This net is so dense that water falling onto the ground is unable to penetrate – so we have a strip of land which is dense with mycelia allowing little else in due to reasons of space; we also have the same patch of land which is suffering from a vastly reduced amount of water. The overall effect of these two things is that plants are unable to grow in that small section, leading to a denuded section of the landscape. Fairy rings are caused by fungi, not fairies. Mind if this was Germany and not Newcastle, we'd have been talking about dragons flying in small circles to produce fairy rings!

PUFF BALLS

In many of the green spaces of Newcastle fungi abound. As well as the fairy rings at Jesmond there are plenty of puffballs as well. A puffball is a type of fungus totally unlike your average mushroom or toadstool. In size and shape they most resemble small stones or pebbles (apart

Puff Balls or the Devil's Snuffbox.

from giant puffballs which are so large that they have been mistaken for sheep – but alas no records of giant puffballs in Newcastle), but in reality they are just as much fungi as the more famous mushrooms, toadstools and moulds. Like their famous counterparts they can appear pretty quickly once the weather conditions are appropriate and equally naturally this sudden appearance has led to some paranormal explanations. For some, puffballs are signs that the devil has been abroad in a particular area. When young, a puffball can be cut open and it is found to have firm, solid white flesh, but when aged this white degenerates into a brown powdery mass. This brown powder is actually the spores of the fungus and at the same time the outer skin changes from an almost rubbery texture to a thin, paper-like consistency. All in all they look just like a little bag of brown powder, a brown powder held in paper. In times past, people believed that old puffballs were bags of snuff that had been dropped as someone was heading over the open grassland in haste. This usually happened overnight so who would be moving around over night, in great haste, perhaps dropping materials? Well no one but the Devil himself, so one of the old names for puffballs was the Devil's Snuffbox.

eight

NEWCASTLE MISCELLANY

THE VAMPIRE RABBIT OF NEWCASTLE

One of the most singular, strange and ultimately beautiful objects to be found in Newcastle is the so-called Vampire Rabbit.

Amen Corner is immediately behind St Nicholas' Cathedral and of the many doorways there, one, 27 Dean Street, belongs to a firm of solicitors and above the door there is a fanged and clawed rabbit, a vampire rabbit if you will. The building was completed in 1901 and it was the work of designers Oliver, Leeson and Wood. Despite much research and digging the origins of the rabbit are unknown. No one is even able to pin down an exact date for the first appearance of the vampire rabbit, though obviously it must be 1901 or later. One thing that has been said about the vampire rabbit is that after an accident, the rabbit's ears were put on incorrectly, changing it from a hare to a rabbit!

In 2008 the rabbit was repainted, changing it from a nice grey rabbit, albeit with fangs and blood red claws, to a black and altogether more evil looking beast.

BALL LIGHTNING

Those living in Newcastle are no doubt used to a bit of bad weather but how many have encountered the ball lightening? Ball lightning is a mysterious form of lightning which is still little understood. For many years it was ignored by scientists and regarded by many as a mere myth. Ball lightning is usually spherical in shape (hence the name) and it can vary in size from that of a pea through to several metres in diameter. Ball lightning can last for several seconds and during this time it can move around, often slowly and looking almost as if controlled by an intelligence. It has also been reported to pass through solid objects without any harm to either lightning or object and yet it has also been blamed for a number of deaths and fires over the years. On one notable occasion ball lighting was even reported to have materialised inside a plane in mid flight.

In the late nineteenth century we have the following report of what claims to be the first photograph of ball lightning:

The Vampire Rabbit – old paint style.

The Vampire Rabbit – new paint style.

Mr Cowper Ranyard, the British scientist, who is making a collection of photographs of lightning flashes, has recently obtained a very remarkable one from an amateur photographer of Newcastle-on-Tyne. It is a perfect image of one of the rarest of electric phenomena – a clear-cut flash of 'ball lightning.' It is said to be the only photograph of such a thing ever made. The luminous spot on the plate bears a strong resemblance to the disk of a sunflower, being a plain circle of light, surrounded by numerous tongues of flame shooting from the periphery of the wheel in every direction. Besides the image of the main flash, the plate is streaked and speckled with many smaller luminosities, supposed to be pictures of stray points of electricity that have separated from the main ball.

This report is rather bizarrely quoted from the *Daily Picayune de New Orlean* (Louisiana) of 3 December 1894; unfortunately no photograph actually accompanied the article.

But this wasn't the only reported occurrence of ball lightning in Newcastle: at the start of the nineteenth century in 1809 David Sutton experienced ball lightning and he thought he was safe in his own home! Lightning struck the chimney of his home and then those assembled in the house saw a globe of fire at the door. The fire ball remained stationary and then moved towards the middle of the room they were in. Once there it exploded into a series of fragments with the noise of a rocket. Fortunately no one was hurt.

But ball lightning has been seen much more recently than the nineteenth century – 1987 is the most modern Newcastle report.

Ian (surname withheld) was eight at the time of the event, but the incident is seared on his memory to this day. He was glued to the window watching a thunderstorm (as eight-year-old children are wont to do) when he saw a bright orange ball. It was travelling at an angle of 50° and heading towards the ground. Ian felt it was very close and travelling slowly, there was no way to compare it in size to known objects, but Ian's gut feeling was that it was small, perhaps about 4in in diameter. Ian describes it as looking like a meteorite with a corona and a small tail. When it disappeared Ian told his parents what he had seen and they went out to investigate, but they were unable to find anything.

Staying with unusual weather, on the night of 29 March 1826, a lunar rainbow was seen for two hours starting at sometime between 8 and 9 p.m. The stars were bright, there was no moon and no clouds and the lunar rainbow was an arch of light clearly defined going from west to east and it extended over the whole city. It must be stressed that the descriptions are of solid light in the same location, so it is unlikely to be a display of the Northern Lights.

TOADS WHERE TOADS OUGHT NOT TO BE

On 18 November 1812 a group of workmen at Bykerhill found a curious thing. They were splitting a block of stone, some three tons in weight, when they found a live toad in the middle. Upon examination the rock proved to have a cavity the same size and shape as the toad and despite minute examination no passageway leading to the cavity could be found. The toad was described as being covered in a black, moist substance. History does not record what happened to the toad. Preserved toads of this nature, whilst not common, are not unheard of and in fact the Booth Museum of Natural History, Brighton, has a mummified toad that was found in a nodule of flint.

HONESTY

Some research, carried out by Melissa Bateson at Newcastle University, is not really paranormal, but is none the less curious.

A poster of drink prices was placed in a canteen in Newcastle University and next to it was an honesty box where people could deposit their payments. The background of the poster alternated between two images during the ten weeks of the trial. One image was a neutral picture of flowers; the other was of a pair of eyes looking directly at the observer. At the end of each week the amount of drinks consumed and the money collected were tallied up. People paid nearly three times the amount of money when the eyes were being used as to when the flower poster was on display. Subconsciously people were thinking they were being watched and overall there was a lack of flower power!

ARCHAEOLOGICAL NEWCASTLE

Archaeologically Newcastle must have all manner of paranormal evidence entombed as part of its 2,000-year history. A recently uncovered 1,800-year-old coffin was found to contain the headless body of a child. Upon examination it transpired that the head had been removed post-mortem and deliberately placed elsewhere within the coffin. It is believed that this was carried out to ensure the unfortunate child did not haunt the living. This is a theme common in vampire lore. This and another coffin discovered at the same time will be on display in the new Great North Museum. Also of Roman origin is the skeleton of a Roman soldier who was in excess of 7ft tall.

Hancock Museum with building work for the construction of the new Great North Museum.

PARANORMAL NEWCASTLE IN LITERATURE

Recognising the paranormal aspects of Newcastle, graphic-novel hero John Constantine had some of his earliest adventures there. Constantine was actually from Liverpool and when the movie version of the *Hellblazer* comics was produced Hollywood bosses decided that Keanu Reeves would be the perfect choice to play the demon slayer. Naturally in this film version all mention of Newcastle is removed. In the Hellblazer mythos much is made of an early séance in Newcastle which went badly wrong, unleashing many of the demons Constantine himself had to subsequently fight.

SPONTANEOUS HUMAN COMBUSTION

Spontaneous Human Combustion (SHC) is the apparent and (usually) complete burning of an individual with no obvious start mechanism for the fire. Many people dismiss it as merely someone falling asleep near a naked flame, but the reality of the recorded cases is somewhat different. SHC is characterised by a victim's body being completely destroyed by fire whilst at the same time many flammable items nearby remaining undamaged. Often paper and furniture are undamaged by the fire but there is frequently encountered a fatty deposit on all items nearby.

In 1853 Charles Dickens was so sure of the existence of the phenomenon that he included a death by SHC in *Bleak House*, this event was inspired by the real life death of the Countess Bandi of Cesena in 1731. A *Christmas Carol* and *Great Expectations* also make reference to a case of SHC.

And there is an SHC case from Newcastle reported from North Terrace on the 16 December 1859. Ann Ridley worked as an assistant in a pharmacist's shop and lived in the premises of her employer. Whilst attending to her employer's wife, Ann's dress burst into flames. All present in the house attempted to extinguish the flames but initially to no avail. A passing dentist named Markham tried to help but he merely found Ann ablaze and in such a state that he could 'hardly believe he was looking at a human being.' At this point Ridley was still alive and with the help of Markham they were eventually able to put out the flames. First aid was given and Ridley was taken to the nearest hospital. Ridley was clearly aware of the seriousness of the situation as she made her last wish known: she desired to be buried in St Edmund's churchyard of Gateshead. And she duly was.

IT'S RAINING DONKEYS

As well as hosting paranormal events and phenomena some truly bizarre things have taken place at the Castle Keep. Chief amongst these has to be the tale of the flying donkey.

In 1733 an entrepreneur had worked out how to make a bit of money: a demonstration of the first human-powered flight! The ideal place for this was to fly from the top of the Keep – soaring majestically over the heads of everyone and heading towards the River Tyne he was sure to impress all and then a path would be beaten to his door as he sold his own flying machines. The flying machine, or more accurately the set of wings he was about to strap to his back, was actually quite heavy so he employed a donkey to help him carry it to the top of the Keep, all 100ft of it. For anyone who has visited the view from the top is truly breathtaking, but you may think differently if you know you that are about to throw yourself off the top in a few minutes, with an untested flying machine strapped to your back. Our entrepreneur decided that discretion was the better part of valour and that he would not throw himself to what he now felt would be certain doom. But what about the crowds milling around at the bottom of the Keep? They had come for a performance and spectacle and if he tried to leave without entertaining them the results would surely be the same as if he had thrown himself from the top! And then he remembered his good and faithful donkey; his good, faithful and expendable donkey. Quicker than a flash he strapped the flying wings to the donkey and pushed it off the top of the Keep. Gravity got the better of the situation and the donkey plunged to the bottom of the tower. Where it miraculously survived! Which is more then can be said for the spectator who cushioned the fall of the donkey…

PHANTOM BLACK DOGS

In the UK there are many traditions of Phantom Black Dogs and many have their own names, for example Black Shuck, the Capelthwaite, Mauthe Doo, Padfoot or barguest.

Going far enough back in history it can be seen that the black dog (the fairy hound) is present in Celtic mythology and is often seen as a precursor of death. It is possible that barguest is a corruption of barrow ghost – a ghost of a dog which appears from a fairy mound

View from the Castle Keep looking towards the River Tyne, the last view the donkey had before being thrown off the roof.

or barrow (an ancient burial site). The barguest can actually bring about death as it is said to have a venomous paw and anyone struck with it will die. According to J. Brand writing in 1777 in *Observations on Popular Antiquities* the streets of Newcastle were haunted by a barguest which took the form of a mastiff. Sometimes just to confuse matters a barguest could take the form of headless man or woman, a black cat or even a white rabbit! One later appearance of a barguest was described in *A Memoir of Robert Surtees* by George Taylor, Robert Surtees and James Rain of 1852, but this one was quite frankly the sort of thing it would be useful to have around:

> At Newcastle he was a friendly daemon, devoted to the service of the whole community; swam the river for a midwife; did the work of the servants; and, in short, performed all the offices of a public brownie.'

A brownie was a house spirit or if you prefer a house elf of the type featured in *Harry Potter* (Dobby). 'I have, indeed, heard that he now and then gave a drunkard or night wander a severe fright by rolling before them like a ball of fire, staring with saucer eyes.'

Walter Scott makes brief mention of the Mayor of Newcastle owning a barguest which amuses itself by rolling canon balls around the city!

PARANORMAL MUSEUM DISPLAYS

The staff of the Newcastle-based museums service are an imaginative lot and not afraid to venture into the realms of the paranormal. For example from the end of 2002 to January 2003 artist (and crop-circle manufacturer) Rod Dickinson, in conjunction with the Tyne and Wear Museums Technical Team and Headway Community Theatre Group, created an Air Loom for display in the Laing Art Gallery. But what is an Air Loom?

To answer that question we have to travel to London of 1810 where one James Tilly Matthews was incarcerated in Bedlam, the asylum which has given its name to all noisy and confused states. Matthews was a man ahead of his time in many respects. He claimed that his actions were being controlled not by him, but by a strange implant in his head. This implant was controlled by a gang who operated through the devices of an electromagnetic machine. Matthews claimed that there were many such groups in operation, and the one responsible for his maladies was called the Air Loom Gang. The gang were responsible for implanting thoughts into his head – a practice he called kiteing, stopping him from speaking ('fluid locking'), cutting his circulation ('sudden death squeezing') and 'brain lengthening' which would 'cause good sense to appear as insanity, and convert truth to libel.' The case was publicised by John Halam who was then the apothecary at Bedlam. The book he wrote goes by the rather snappy title of *Illustrations of Madness: Exhibiting a Singular Case of Insanity, And a No Less Remarkable Difference in Medical Opinions: Developing the Nature of An Assailment, And the Manner of Working Events; with a Description of Tortures Experienced by Bomb-Bursting, Lobster-Cracking and Lengthening the Brain. Embellished with a Curious Plate.*

So Dickinson and friends recreated the air loom for a museum, based on the descriptions and sketches that Matthews had produced and which Halam had included in his book. The mind-control machine was not a subtle piece of equipment – it was constructed of oak,

The Air Loom: A Human Influencing Machine. (Courtesy of Rod Dickinson)

brass and leather and measured 10m by 10m by 6m. Matthews described how the machine ran on magnetic fluids (which were believed to be responsible for hypnotism and were a popular explanation for many things at the time). He further went on to explain that skilled pneumatic chemists would operate the machine, bending the character of the fluids, and that these warped fluids would then travel towards and influence their intended victim. The Air Loom was to be used for nefarious purposes on MPs and inmates of asylums. As far as we know the Newcastle showing is the first ever manufacture of such a device unless of course Matthews was correct in his statements. And if he was indeed correct then one wonders what Rod Dickinson was up to in Newcastle at the end of 2002 and beginning of 2003...

WHERE TO NOW?

So you've seen that Newcastle is a truly paranormal city – what can you do to get more involved?

The Centre for Life is a good place to start. When it was being built some 300 skeletons were found in the grounds and security guards reported all sorts of strange feelings, from being watched through to overwhelming feelings that there were people present in areas which were quite patently empty. The hauntings appear to have stopped since the completion of the building, but another phenomenon has moved in, that of the Paranormal Conference. In 2007 a whole weekend was devoted to cryptozoology: a weekend of talks and an exhibition called

Newcastle Centre for Life, some hauntings but some paranormal conferences too.

Interactive ghost tour.

Myths and Monsters. Myths and Monsters had local tales of giant worms from the Lambton Worm to the South Shields Shonie, tales of imaginary animals inhabiting zoos and stories of mermaids in art. Then in 2008 as part of their Keeping up with the (Indiana) Jones family weekend there were a number of presentations on the reality behind the Crystal Skull from the 2008 film, *Indiana Jones and the Kingdom of the Crystal Skull*. As part of this weekend the Centre for Life even had a genuine crystal skull on display! Definitely a place to watch.

In 2009 a Fortean Society (named after American collector of oddities Charles Fort) opened up monthly lectures in different pubs on all different aspects of the paranormal.

For those wanting to do a bit more, active ghost and witch tours are available at the weekend courtesy of Alone in the Dark Entertainment.

And for the serious researcher of the paranormal there is even a course to learn all of the appropriate techniques – and for good measure it's based in the rather splendid Castle Garth (Castle Keep). This course is also from Alone in the Dark Entertainment, a group set up by Steve Taylor in 2007. Steve describes himself as a local horror historian and he uses a range of ghost-hunting equipment, all of which are available to try out during his various haunted diversions.

If you want to get involved in practical investigations and overnight vigils then there are various charity events at supposed haunted locations. Most of these are not serious investigations and should be regarded as a bit of fun whilst helping a good cause.

If you want a serious investigation then organisations such as Otherworld North East and Paranormal UK are groups with an active investigation schedule. Otherworld North East has a good website as well, complete with a discussion forum which can be used to get to know people and to find out what events are taking place.

Learning how to hunt ghosts.

Railing decoration showing castle motif.

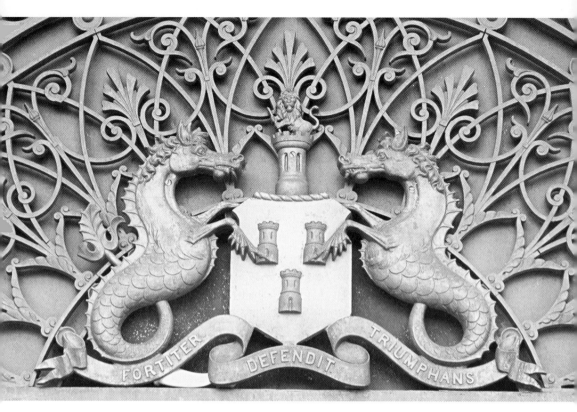

Newcastle coat of arms supported by sea horses: linking the New Castle with the importance that the sea has had for the development of the city.

One thing that should be pointed out is that Newcastle is slowly starting to embrace its paranormal heritage and to lose its embarrassed about it. Ghost and witch tours, courses, clubs and groups and an ever-increasing range of events centred around Halloween are just the start.

To keep up with all of the latest developments and an opportunity to let me know about your paranormal Newcastle experiences you could of course visit the dedicated Paranormal Newcastle section at www.gordonrutter.com.

BIBLIOGRAPHY

Armstrong, Pamela *Dark Tales of Old Newcastle* (Bridge Studios, 1990)

Bath, Jo *Dancing With the Devil and other True Tales of Northern Witchcraft* (Tyne Bridge Publishing, 2002)

Histon, Vanessa *Ghosts of Grainger Town* (Tyne Bridge Publishing)

Histon, Vanessa *Nightmare on Grey Street* (Tyne Bridge Publishing, 2000)

Liddell, Tony *Otherworld North East – Ghosts and Hauntings Explored* (Tyne Bridge Publishing, 2004)

Reynolds, H. *The Body in the Bank: Famous Northern Murders* (Sandhill Press Ltd, 1990)

Ritson, Darren *Haunted Newcastle* (The History Press, 2009)

Stead, W.T. *Real Ghost Stories* (Grant Richards, 1891)

Whatever you do and however you intend to continue your look at Paranormal Newcastle, have a good time and remember there is a lot to take in and a lot to do, but above all, remember to enjoy yourself!

Quayside with Sunday Market.

Other titles published by The History Press

Paranormal West Yorkshire
ANDY OWENS

This richly illustrated book covers a fascinating range of strange events, from famous cases such as the Cottingley Fairies – a mystery which puzzled countless investigators (including Sir Arthur Conan Doyle) – to hauntings in West Yorkshire's pubs, manor houses and private residences and apparitions such as the Pontefract Poltergeist. With eyewitness accounts of big cats and UFOs and sources both ancient and modern this book will delight all lovers of the mysterious and the paranormal.

978 0 7524 4810 7

Haunted Newcastle
DARREN W. RITSON

This creepy collection of true-life tales takes the reader on a tour through the streets, cemeteries, alehouses, and attics of Newcastle. Drawing on historical and contemporary sources and containing many tales which have never before been published, it unearths a chilling range of supernatural phenomena, including the vampire rabbit of Collingwood House, the Pink Lady of Jesmond and the tale of the mysterious witches' bones.

978 0 7524 4880 0

Haunted Sunderland
RUPERT MATTHEWS

Explore Sunderland's darkest secrets with this creepy collection of true-life tales from ghost-hunter Rupert Matthews. Containing many tales which have never before been published, it unearths a chilling range of supernatural phenomena, from the Ryhope Poltergeist and the White Lady of Washington Hall to the glowing grave at Wingate and the spectral talking cat.

978 0 7524 4663 9

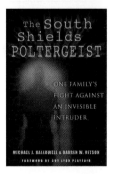

South Shields Poltergeist
MICHAEL J. HALLOWELL & DARREN W. RITSON

In December 2005 a family began to experience poltergeist-like phenomena in their home. Slowly but steadily the phenomena escalated, and in July 2006 the authors were asked to investigate. This book is a chilling diary of an ongoing poltergeist case which the authors believe rivals any previously documented.

978 0 7509 4874 6

Visit our website and discover thousands of other History Press books.

www.thehistorypress.co.uk

The
History
Press